To Jane

Peace is

Jim Byars

A Call to Wholeness

Empowering Organizations through Possibility

Jan Byars, PhD & Susan Taylor

Copyright © 2021 Jan Byars, PhD & Susan Taylor.

All rights reserved. No part of this book may be used or reproduced by any means, graphic, electronic, or mechanical, including photocopying, recording, taping or by any information storage retrieval system without the written permission of the authors except in the case of brief quotations embodied in critical articles and reviews.

This book is a work of non-fiction. Unless otherwise noted, the author and the publisher make no explicit guarantees as to the accuracy of the information contained in this book and in some cases, names of people and places have been altered to protect their privacy.

Balboa Press books may be ordered through booksellers or by contacting:

Balboa Press
A Division of Hay House
1663 Liberty Drive
Bloomington, IN 47403
www.balboapress.com
844-682-1282

Because of the dynamic nature of the Internet, any web addresses or links contained in this book may have changed since publication and may no longer be valid. The views expressed in this work are solely those of the author and do not necessarily reflect the views of the publisher, and the publisher hereby disclaims any responsibility for them.

The author of this book does not dispense medical advice or prescribe the use of any technique as a form of treatment for physical, emotional, or medical problems without the advice of a physician, either directly or indirectly. The intent of the author is only to offer information of a general nature to help you in your quest for emotional and spiritual well-being. In the event you use any of the information in this book for yourself, which is your constitutional right, the author and the publisher assume no responsibility for your actions.

Photo cover by Diane Elliott ALL RIGHTS RESERVED

From Integral Meditation, by Ken Wilber, ©2016 by Ken Wilber. Reprinted by arrangement with Shambhala Publications, Inc., Boulder, CO., www.shambhala.com.

Jan's head shot by Jennifer Soots
Susan's head shot by Christy McCombie

Print information available on the last page.

ISBN: 978-1-9822-7666-9 (sc)
ISBN: 978-1-9822-7668-3 (hc)
ISBN: 978-1-9822-7667-6 (e)

Library of Congress Control Number: 2021922585

Balboa Press rev. date: 11/24/2021

Praise for *A Call to Wholeness*

Shifting from fragmentation to Wholeness is critical to sustain humanity and our planet and requires unwavering commitment to first take a deeper look at ourselves. There are powerful tools and practices at our disposal that help us to create new realities. Begin now. Novice or a master, A Call to Wholeness *will serve you in your personal and professional journey—time and time again.*

Joseph Jaworski
Chairman, Generon International

Good fairy tales allow us to suspend belief long enough to learn a lesson or two. This work does just that. This is a very impressive compilation and evolution of modern leadership perspectives that go well beyond hierarchical models, which are based on gaining and wielding authority. Reflective leaders in any organizational setting would benefit from slowing down a bit, learning from a talking dog and maybe seeing a bit of themselves in the fictional lives of others.

Anthony Scriffignano
Senior Vice President and Chief Data Scientist
Dun & Bradstreet

Susan and Jan bring a fresh and well-researched perspective to workplace consciousness. While Bohm's ideas are central, A Call to Wholeness *incorporates wisdom from the giants of science, philosophy, religion, and corporate leadership. A* Call to Wholeness *stretched me both as a leader and as a human being.*

Christopher Willis
Chief People Officer, PrimeSource Building Products
Former Chief Legal, People and Corporate Affairs Officer for Interstate Batteries
Adjunct Professor of Advanced Coaching and Leadership at Southern Methodist University

How do you speak of leadership and the inner journey necessary to lead? This book is an excellent resource that invites the reader into an experience with leadership and inner growth that doesn't lecture—it offers and invites. It is especially well suited for those looking for shared leadership and cooperation in a work environment using 21st century understanding of neuroscience, spiritual traditions, and leadership theory.

Rebecca Parker, M.Div.
Director, Mary & Martha's Place

We are in a constant search back to Wholeness right after we emerge from our meditative state in the womb into this complex, fragmented world with all its conflicting demands, enticement, and fears that play uniquely on every individual. A Call to Wholeness immediately comes across as an important and urgent message about that search, and for me it was a reminder that freedom from strife can be quite simple and achievable. We individually and collectively have all the capabilities inside us to complete that search.

Susan and Jan weave an entertaining narrative that reminded me of Jonathan Livingston Seagull. The themes and backdrop are immediately relatable to today's corporate professional context, and as you live through the character's evolution, you draw lessons about control, power, leadership and positive change that are clear. Every professional will benefit from reading this important Call!

Rajiv Singh
Co-Chair FoodShot Global
Former CEO, Rabobank North America

A Call to Wholeness is a refreshing addition to the global literature on transformative leadership. Told as a story, it is digested differently than the conceptual nonfiction that has been the popular form of published wisdom. This tale could have some significant impact in transforming the field of organizational leadership.

John Renesch
Futurist
Award-winning Author
Conscious Leadership Pioneer

Fairy tales can come true, it can happen to you
If you are young at heart
For it's hard, you will find, to be narrow of mind
If you are young at heart

Frank Sinatra

Jan Byars

To Melody, Karen, and Matthias for all your loving support

Susan Taylor

To my children, Carolanne and Erin, for the light
and joy they continuously bring to my life

Contents

In Gratitude xiii

Foreword xv

Introduction xxi

Part One: A Call to Wholeness 1

Part Two: Living into Wholeness: The Journey 107

Appendix A: Resources 135

Appendix B: Outline of Process 142

Appendix C: Glossary 145

Index 151

Contact Us 155

About the Authors 157

In Gratitude

First and foremost, our deepest gratitude and respect to David Bohm for his seminal work, which has deeply touched our lives and the lives of so many others who are on the journey to heal fragmentation, prejudice, and imbalance through coherence, shared meaning, unity, and Wholeness.

A very deep bow of appreciation to Joseph Jaworski, for compelling work on what it means to lead first from inside, at the heart of creativity and deep knowing. Joseph has been an inspiration to us through his books, *Synchronicity* and *Source*. We are deeply grateful for Joseph's support and unwavering enthusiasm to endorse our book and write the Foreword.

Deep appreciation and gratitude to our readers, Karen Buckley, Rebecca Parker, Karen Friss, Laura Santana, Anthony Scriffignano, Christopher Sanchez Lascurain, Erin Taylor, and Richard Taylor for their tireless effort to read and review early manuscripts. Your continued support has been valuable beyond words.

We are very grateful to Diane Elliott for the cover photo of the Santiago Trail and again to Christopher Sanchez Lascurain for our book video.

A heartfelt tip of our hats to all of our endorsers who—despite busy schedules and full lives—took time to read our manuscript and share their praise for our work.

Sharing gratitude also to Kim Byas who helped us to refine the voice of Calvin. And to Stephanie Gunning who meticulously proofread the final manuscript just prior to the final submission to our publisher.

A generous shout out to Christopher Walsh for his continued care, patience, and support with the authors, as they spent endless hours writing, editing, and refining in the dining room of his and Susan's home.

A big hug of appreciation and pat on the head to Molly, who became our muse for the main character of this book.

And finally, but certainly not least, many thanks to all the ladies who served Jan iced tea at Boulder Creek.

Thank you all so very much from the bottom of our hearts. It is people like you, along with others who are mentioned amid the pages of this book, that continue to inspire and encourage us to stay the path. We are eternally grateful to you all.

Jan and Susan
2021

Foreword

Many of you may smile, as you realize this story to be a fairy tale . . . but there is truth and power in myth.

As in most fairy tales, you will experience villains. And heroines . . . set in a fantastic backdrop that combines real life and the magic of an enchanted forest, sometimes feeling close to home and at other times feeling far, far away.

The story is short. It is also powerful.

There are no dragons, but there are demons.

Where lessons are learned through wonderous elixir. And problems are solved, but not with three wishes. And not everyone lives happily ever after.

Or do they…?

My contact with this book also begins as a story. Perhaps more fantasy than fairy tale. More crisis than happily ever after. And no doubt, an adventure.

Looking back at the first half of my life, it's difficult for me to understand how I could have maintained such a fragmented existence for so long without caving in to its incoherence and lack of central commitment. Life was an absolute blur—I was popping from one activity to another without a moment's hesitation to become silent, reflect and consider my overall life direction.

At the time, I considered my life to be a great life, but in fact, I really didn't know life at all. Mine was a Disney World sort of life—inauthentic, narrow, utterly predictable, and largely devoid of any real meaning.

The end to this illusion came to me—as it does for so many others—by means of a personal crisis. It was 1975. I was forty-one years old. I had just returned to Houston from Circle J Ranch, having spent the Thanksgiving weekend with my father and some business associates. Just as I was walking into my study to put down my gear, my wife asked me to sit down, stating she had something important to tell me. She wanted a divorce.

This news came to me as a complete surprise. And while I don't remember much about the conversation that night due to the state of shock I was in, the overriding feeling was a complete and utter sense of devastation and despair. My marriage of twenty years was over—period, end of paragraph!

There are many types of life crises; mine was a divorce—something that caused more emotional upheaval than I ever could have imagined with deep feelings of powerlessness and isolation. Yet it also inspired me the infamous *wake up call* that caused me to reevaluate my life. It shook me to the core, forcing me to look into myself. And in many ways, I didn't like what I saw.

I began to reflect upon how I was living, where I was heading, and what I wanted out of life. I started writing in a journal. I was reading—a lot—and for the first time, thinking deeply about personal and philosophical issues.

I talked to people—people my age or older—discovering that most in my generation who had achieved a great measure of success were feeling equally to how I was feeling. They were not truly living life. They were not truly free. They wanted to step out and make a difference—to contribute. But instead, they were mobilized by fear and the need to "have" instead of "be."

In all of this, what I *truly* discovered was that people are not really afraid to die. They are afraid of not ever having lived, never having deeply considered their higher purpose.

As we consider our current circumstances, nothing has categorically changed for most of us. We remain in a trap of overactivity—with no time or energy to seize the extraordinary opportunities life presents to us. This has most certainly been amplified by all we've endured this past year—this year we call 2020.

And once again, I look back only to realize that this is the beginning of yet another new life journey—the only journey that remains constant: the inner journey.

"We have phenomenal capacities within us, if we only knew how to access them."

—David Bohm

We've all had those moments of crisis. We've also all had those moments when things come together in extraordinary ways—when events that could never be predicted, let alone controlled, remarkably seem to guide us along our path. The closest I've come to finding a word for what happens in these moments is "synchronicity."

My quest to understand synchronicity arose out of a series of events in my life that led me into a process of inner transformation.

Such is the same with this book.

A Call to Wholeness builds directly on all of my thinking over forty-five years and goes further to penetrate deeper insights into leading as a way of being.

Why is it that some organizations mire in internal strife while others inspire and challenge their stakeholders toward creativity and growth? How does leadership influence organizational culture? These are not new questions, but to date, we struggle for the answers. Jan and Susan draw from their combined fifty-plus years of experience in leadership development and organizational transformation, exploring deeper aspects of these and other ideas in a whimsical, practical way. Underpinned by David Bohm's understanding of Undivided Wholeness and Dialogue, their shared account reveals what it means to accept each other as legitimate human beings.

The result is a most unusual book—rare at best among business books—perhaps even unprecedented. This may present challenges for readers used to "expert" accounts, scientific "proof," and "academic" theories. Yet Jan and Susan's understandings are profound. How else could you take some of the most complex theories and concepts around leadership and quantum physics and turn them into a fairy tale? It was Albert Einstein who said, "If you can't explain it simply, **you don't understand it well enough.**" I am struck by this book's simplicity and clarity.

Susan and I are business partners, working together now for more than twenty-five years. Not only is she the CEO of Generon International, but also as a coach and consultant, she has devoted two decades of life-energy in service to helping others fulfill their deeper purpose, as she fosters creative and inspiring business environments that support human growth and development. Through years of individual practice and personal discipline, Susan has refined her capacity for other ways of knowing that supersede the ordinary, which makes her quite extraordinary in this field and *the expert* in Bohmian Dialogue, exploring and practicing Dialogue in the way Bohm envisioned.

My relationship with Jan is newer and certainly not less profound. Jan's work with individuals and organizations centers on field theory, value-based leadership and the physical and psychological aspects leadership and change. She has a strong educational background, and personally, has a deeply embedded centering practice.

She has integrated critical intrapersonal capacities into purpose-driven leadership and organizational development. She helps leaders create and hold the environment for transformational, sustainable change. Jan does this by helping leaders significantly increase their self-awareness and self-regulation, shifting out of their own limitations and expanding their capacity and perception. She helps leaders to dramatically increase clarity and alignment, as they develop their capacity for conscious leadership.

Bohm spoke to fragmentation and wholeness as "especially important to consider . . . for fragmentation is now very widespread, not only throughout society, but also in each individual; and this is leading to a kind of general confusion of the mind, which creates an endless series of problems and interferes with our clarity of perception so seriously as to prevent us from being able to solve most of them."

When I met David Bohm in 1980, he taught me that the world is fundamentally inseparable, proving through Bell's theorem that oneness exists—that everything is connected to everything else and that there is "separation without separateness." This is how the universe is constructed; "the oneness implicit in Bell's theorem envelops human beings and atoms alike."

And yet so much fragmentation exists in our lives.

I am now deeply troubled by the state of the world, hoping it's not too late to begin to heal the fragmentation of the planet. Few times in my life have I experienced the human condition challenged on such a global scale. I do, however, remain confident about the extraordinary potential and capacity we have for navigating change, as we transition through these chaotic times.

Don't do what I did. Learn from my experience. I hope you won't look back only to question how you could have maintained such a fragmented existence. Shifting from fragmentation to Wholeness requires unwavering commitment to take a deeper look at ourselves. There are powerful tools and practices at our disposal that help us to create new realities. Begin now. Novice or a master, this book will serve you in your own personal journey—time and time again.

Joseph Jaworski
Wimberley, Texas
April 17, 2021

Introduction

This is a story about Wholeness, a story about accepting power and recognizing possibility. It is written at the archetypal level where net worth and thousands of followers have no meaning. It offers a new paradigm for life and business. One that replaces the tale of fear in which we currently live; one that replaces the belief that life and work has to be a struggle.

> *Fragmentation and wholeness: It is especially important to consider this today, for fragmentation is now very widespread, not only throughout society, but also in each individual; and this is leading to a kind of general confusion of the mind, which creates an endless series of problems and interferes with our clarity of perception so seriously as to prevent us from being able to solve most of them.*
> David Bohm, *Wholeness and the Implicate Order*

Living in a fragmented state changes us. It changes how our hearts function, how our brains are wired; it changes our bodies. Most of us know this in terms of feeling overwhelmed and burned out. We know the words, but don't really understand the impact on our lives, our work, and the people around us. And we have even less awareness of how it impacts our organizations.

We live with a "general confusion of our mind," brought on by intensity, complexity, and fragmentation. Most of believe this is just the way it is . . . it will never change . . . head down, suck it up, and get through it. This is the driving masculine energy that has run our western world for millennia. This worldview has us analyzing and cutting everything to the smallest common denominator, reducing to smaller and smaller pieces, forgetting that Wholeness even exists.

The old system has such a strong grip, it operates nearly invisibly. It will take a leap of faith and willingness to find a new way to step out of it. Do you hear it? There is a call to Wholeness. People are beginning to long for a different way of being.

This book is written from a softer, more feminine energy. One that is more receptive and accepts and encourages intellectual curiosity and creativity. It allows for integrating instead of fragmenting.

In fact, integrated within our story is the literature from many fields of study with special emphasis on the ideas of physicist, David Bohm.

We need to begin to step out of all this mania, to soothe our cells and release the stored trauma from our lives. We need to be more centered and allow more rest. From this place of deeper peace, we become gathered in our hearts. We expand our ability to see patterns and anticipate obstacles. Receptivity is the opposite of the typical driving, pushing mode we have all been taught.

Our story begins in a hypermanic world of work where the only criterion for success is money, even as we sacrifice our relationships, our health, and our planet. This is a fictional account of a nonfiction process. Part one is a story of transformation, first individually and then as an organization. Part two offers a more analytical version of the process and the resources we used.

This story considers a reality of coherence and order, where interconnection is primary, and our decisions and actions have the profound impact we intend. One where science and creativity come together to bring out our best selves. Where we can take the time to work for our common good, incorporating our communities and allowing Wholeness to reemerge.

In the Appendixes, you will find some of our favorite resources, an outline of the process discovered by Gertrude and Laura, and a glossary of terms.

This story is written from the heart, where Wholeness already resides. We have been trained to see our hearts as weak and have learned to cut ourselves off from our emotions. We have been taught to be fearful of our heart's wisdom. And yet, our hearts have no fear of our minds, with no need to cut out our capacity to think. Our hearts hold wisdom, look for interconnection, and are able to integrate our knowledge, experience, and training.

We invite you to stay in your heart, allowing the deepest meaning of our story to emerge. We invite you to suspend and allow a new perspective.

Many of you may laugh, as you realize this story to be a fairy tale … but there is truth and power in myth.

Our story is short. It is also powerful.

There are no dragons, but there are demons.

There are no unicorns, but there is a talking dog.

Where lessons are learned through wonderous elixir. And problems are solved, but not with three wishes. And not everyone lives happily ever after.

Or do they?

Written in storybook fashion, underpinned by David Bohm's understanding of Undivided Wholeness and Dialogue, our story is a shared account that reveals what it means to accept each other as legitimate human beings.

This is a tale of transformation. And a new way of being. A story about two women who learn to see, and in so doing, discover a world of joy and beauty. But not without the often-perilous path of self-discovery. It is also about an organization that learns to listen, to be inclusive and act from Wholeness. It's a shero's journey, into the world of chaos and fragmentation, which transforms into color and light through courage, clarity, and intention.

Part One

A Call to Wholeness

The literature and scientific concepts illustrated here are real. Our story is a fictionalized description of our current working world. Being a fairy tale, there is a bit of a magic in our use of time and space. Any names, characters, or incidents are products of the authors' imaginations. Any similarity to actual people or events is coincidental.

Chapter 1

Once upon a time, the stork made a delivery to the wrong house; only, of course, she didn't, as there are no accidents. The baby girl was dropped into a family of women. Yes, there was a father, but he was rarely present. The girls—six to be exact—were dominated by their mother, Rachael.

All of the girls were powerful, beautiful women, but much of their childhood was focused on survival. In this, they had to face their fears, overcome obstacles, and draw from within.

There were many adversities presented for all of them, but specifically for the fifth girl. She was different, not quite like the rest. Her brain worked in an unusual way. She was creative and bright, but never really learned which was her right and which was her left.

The fifth girl also had the capacity to "see." She could see patterns and their meaning beneath the surface. She knew the world was actually different than the way most people experienced it, which caused her a lot of confusion, as no one she knew saw what she saw.

As she grew up and moved away, the fifth girl began to experiment with new and different ways of living. College opened up her world. It was a miracle to even be there; and she no longer struggled in a fog of negativity.

Set free from so many limitations, the fifth girl focused on her goals, her degree, and her professional success. She worked hard and did it all right, graduating a full semester early, beginning her career so much sooner than anticipated. Quickly landing a job at the company where she interned, Gertrude climbed the ladder faster than she ever expected. At just twenty-four, she made her first professional goal: art director of a major market TV station. Wow, six years early!

Gertrude was stunned; she was stunned because ***she hated it.***

I did everything right! I played the game! I worked the plan. Gertrude froze, lost as to what to do. Head down, she walked forward, afraid to make another mistake.

Gertrude was the creative director of Pan American Broadcasting (PanAm). For many years, she struggled to understand the corporate mentality. Every day she went to work, dealing with a reality she did not believe in, working in a place she felt she did not belong. She worked in a world where war metaphors were common and world domination was an actual business goal. There was no insight into our deep connection or our interdependence. It was all conquer and dominate. As long as money was made in the short term, it was a success!

Gertrude had felt the pull to know more deeply for more than a decade now. She had felt a calling to show up differently and to do meaningful work. She spent her free time reading about the newest concepts in leadership and science and even some of the ancient mystical religious texts. There was a great deal of hope in knowing there was another way. It helped her feel sane, it helped her direct her attention toward to a better world.

But at PanAm, it was only about money and control. She sighed as she walked down the hall, *How does anyone get any work done in all this crazy?*

A Call to Wholeness

Friday mornings were the worst because of the required weekly leadership meeting. That day was no exception. Tom Simpson was the director of sales. He was an idiot and the most narcissistic person Gertrude had ever met. He presented the sales plan for the second half of the year. His ideas were based on manipulation and short-term goals, but no one else appeared to see this. Or maybe they did and just didn't care. Or were they too afraid to challenge him?

In meetings, Tom just talked until no one challenged him. He interrupted, disregarded, and outlasted by just repeating the same old crap. Everyone had stopped making any effort, even the SVP. Tom just bullied his way through. And this was supposed to be a value-based organization.

Tom's plan would likely increase sales, but in the long term it would lose money and position for the company. Gertrude had a friend who would have seen this too, a companion in all the nonsense, but she was on vacation. So, Gertrude sighed and counted the minutes until the meeting would end and she could go back to her office. At least it was Friday!

It was Gertrude's department that took the plan and created the sales materials, the copy and graphics. Once again, she was doing something she did not believe in. Something that she knew was wrong, out of integrity with herself, draining all her energy and attention. She knew by now that the world reflected who she was, both personally and professionally. She knew that her integrity and intentions were the driving force for her world. And she knew what she was doing did not line up. The universe was not as she had been told—cold and limited; she had felt the vastness of the Whole. She was tired of being ridiculed for not playing the game. Gertrude felt hopeless.

She also knew that thinking Tom was a narcissistic idiot was wrong. She knew that seeing him as "other," as separate, limited her capacity to see the Whole. Seeing Tom as separate was the same perspective and justification he used to belittle the team.

Operating from within the Whole was where the solution to each problem existed; but she felt unfocused, unable to see how to move forward. The toxicity was suffocating.

Gertrude had been reading about the nature of reality where she learned that—from a quantum perspective—Wholeness and interconnection were primary. Quantum reality does not divide mind from matter, the observer from the observed. It did not divide her from Tom.

She understood that working from Wholeness does not mean that you step out of a situation or make the "out there" world wrong. Quite the contrary, it is about staying in the moment, looking inward. *The only way out is through. And to go through the emotion, to feel the pain I don't want to feel, I have to love myself enough to honor the emotions!* She sat pondering the situation, *What does this really mean? How do you actually live like this? It all feels so abstract and far away.*

The day was *finally* over. Gertrude left work feeling defeated and angry. On her way home, she stopped at her favorite place, Charleston Falls, a beautiful nature reserve—a quiet and enchanted spot free from all the chaos of everyday life. Gertrude changed her shoes, grabbed her water bottle, and began walking into the forest.

She was still caught in the mire of anger and illusion. She struggled with the reality she saw at work—it was like walking in a hall of mirrors, constantly hitting the wall at every turn. She was exhausted.

Finally, she stopped fighting and sat on a log. She surrendered all her pushing and trying to force reality into her own version. As she rested, tears streamed down her face.

A Call to Wholeness

She knew the universe was not as she had been told—cold and limited; she had felt the vastness of the Whole. She was tired of being ridiculed for not playing the game. *Was all this effort for nothing? Am I really not going to be able to find a different way?* She had seen too many glimpses of Wholeness and of peace to believe it did not exist.

She had shared these visions with others, and they laughed. Yet she had seen the miracles of interconnection so many times. *What am I missing? Why is it so hard?* Gertrude sat there for a long time, too tired to get up.

As she stayed quiet, the emotions continued to come. Anger, fear, guilt, and shame ran through her. She felt washed in the physical reality of each state, as she let them come, no longer having the energy to stop them, no longer holding them back. She had looked foolish so many times; what difference did one more time make? For the first time in her life, like ebb and flow, she let her emotions fully expand and then let them go.

As she rested, her breathing became quiet. She felt the rhythm of her breathing shift and her heartbeat slow. She closed her eyes. Her breathing continued to be smoother and deeper. The toxicity of PanAm seemed to slip right out of her.

She felt the warmth of a beautiful light, soft and gentle. It dried her tears, enveloping and filling her with peace. She blinked her eyes to make sure it was really there. *Yes, it was real.* The forest was bathed in luminous color. Her exhaustion gone and her perception changed. Gertrude felt restored and surrounded by love.

Filled with joy and clarity, she felt the light expand. Gertrude was no longer confused. She had a knowing and a sense that there was a way to blend the truth of her heart with the truth of her mind. Confidence restored, Gertrude felt strong and powerful. Once again, she was gifted with peace. In this, she now knew this was her real work and that the position she held was simply a place to begin.

Gertrude stood up and began to walk the trail back to her car. As her eyes were still adjusting, she almost stumbled over a small dog sitting in the middle of the path. He sat there with his eyes twinkling up at her. "Where did you come from? Surely, I would have noticed you sitting there, all this time?"

The dog's tail wagged with joy. He was friendly and clean, snuggling into her touch. He didn't appear lost. Gertrude checked his collar. It read: David Bohm *937-132-4563*. She gave him a pat and let him be. "Go on home, David. I am sure someone is missing you."

Gertrude continued her walk, taking in the beauty and peace of the forest. She felt lighter. She had shaken off all of her stress. That alone was a miracle; it had been a long time since she felt so good.

The dog followed her. When she arrived at her car, he wanted to come too. "I guess it's OK. I'll call your owner when we get home." David Bohm jumped into the back seat like a seasoned traveler. He watched quietly as Gertrude drove home.

After setting out a water bowl, Gertrude called the owner. The number was disconnected. "Huh, that's no good. What are we going to do with you, David Bohm?" The dog looked up with big brown eyes, turning his head, as if he was listening intently.

OK, so browned ground beef it would be for her houseguest's dinner. She would try the Humane Society in the morning.

At bedtime, Gertrude put a blanket down on the floor near her bed where David Bohm curled up and went to sleep.

Gertrude woke the next morning, slowly, in a state of deep calm. She could feel her heart fully expanded, like it was synchronized with love. It pulsed through her, filling her with joy. She knew this feeling well and that this Field of Love is real, always available to us and something she could choose to be aligned with whenever she remembered. *Wow, what a blessing!*

As she rolled over, she came nose to nose with a doggie ready to go outside. After morning snuggles, she roused herself and began her day. The Humane Society agreed to take the dog, but Gertrude couldn't let him be locked up in a cage. So, she left all of her information with the Society, agreeing they would call upon reaching the owner.

Gertrude and her new companion jumped in the car to run the usual Saturday errands and go to the pet store. David was exuberant, pulling her around the store, eagerly helping to find his new bones and toys. It was in this moment, as David Bohm selected yet one more bone that Gertrude decided to call him DB for short. It fit him; and he fit into her life so easily. She loved his quirky ways and especially enjoyed taking him for walks. It broke the cycle of anger and gave her time for peace and quiet.

The next evening, Gertrude returned to the nature reserve with DB. As they walked, she could feel the warmth of the unusual light. Again, joy filled her. *WOW, it's so powerful!* She remembered how just two days before, she started to let go of all the anger; and in doing so, a sense of knowing and peacefulness filled her. That same feeling of connection returned and she basked in it.

As she was leaving and passed the trailhead bulletin board, she saw a sign about a meditation class being offered in the park. *That sounds* perfect! *I could sit in the beauty of the park with DB and be in silence.* Gertrude took a quick picture of the flyer with her cell phone. *Taking a class like this could help me remember Wholeness when I am at work.*

The weekend had flown by, full of joy and quietude and playing with DB. It seemed like everything had slowed down and she had once again found her place. Gertrude felt complete, her world more spacious.

On Monday, Gertrude was hit with a brick wall of anger and frustration, as she walked into the PanAm building. It was like a force field of negative energy. She felt it all the way to her bones. Just breathing the air of this place triggered her. Her peace was gone. And once again she faced what had become her reality—the everyday crazy of the corporate world. It made her nauseous.

Her thoughts began to spin. *This is not the life I want!* Gertrude had been to the trainings and seminars on how it was "supposed to be." But instead . . . what she saw . . . was often an abuse of power through demeaning and derogatory behavior. Good leadership is based in appreciation and making a valuable contribution. The days of command and control were supposed to be gone. A value-based organization is supposed to be built upon relationships—people working together in a noncoercive way, where people could respectfully disagree and work with mutual purpose. Caught in the gap between reality and the way it was "supposed to be" she had made herself sick.

Gertrude knew that PanAm did not operate in the way she knew it could. She knew no matter what skill level or knowledge the leaders had, if trust was lacking, nothing would happen. And she knew nothing good was happening because there was little trust.

This spawned Gertrude's recollection about a book she had read on servant leadership and inward reflection—where problems in the world were viewed as *inside me, not out there*. This all fit with what Gertrude learned about the quantum view of Wholeness and interconnection. But how did it all work?

As a leader in the company, Gertrude's role was supposed to be holding an environment of creativity for her staff, working with them to cocreate and bring forth great ideas and support people like Tom. But how could she create the possibility for all of this with all the public displays of anger, arrogance and contempt? Especially given the way the organization was structured. PanAm's system was set up to pin directors against each other through competition and everyone fighting over the same resources. Shaking her head in dismay, she asked herself, *How had the sales department become my enemy?*

Gertrude was reminded of her everyday reality of chaos and fragmentation—everyone pushing and pulling like a parade of children posing for attention. And when Gertrude left work on Monday evening, she once again felt exhausted—tired of all the games and posturing for power. The joy of the weekend felt foggy—like a distant memory.

As Gertrude opened the door to her house, she was greeted by a wagging tail and welcome eyes. It took only moments before she was on her knees being smothered by slobbery kisses.

Sitting on the floor, DB dancing in delight, Gertrude remembered the weekend and the vision of light and how she felt through its warmth. She realized she had a touchstone to this very special event. *It had to be true; she had DB! Wow! If this was all real, then there had to be a way to live it!* Gertrude made a pact with herself, right then: she would find a way to live reality in the way she knew it could exist!

The rest of the week was lighter. Gertrude had a plan and a new dog. She still had no response from the owner or the Humane Society. But she was happy about that! DB was answering to his nickname and had started sleeping at the end of her bed. He appeared to be very much at home. Gertrude also had adapted; DB was her loving companion, and, like most dog owners, she started talking to him.

"DB, what is the deal with people? Why do they act the way they do? How do I even begin to live the vision shown to me in the forest?" DB wagged his tail, smiling his peculiar doggie smile.

Gertrude and DB had settled into a routine. Every evening, after greeting DB, she went about making dinner and venting about work. After dinner, DB and Gertrude went for long walks, many of them in the forest where they had met. There were no other visions, no unusual events ... just an abiding sense of peacefulness.

When they were walking, Gertrude's stress seemed to fade away. The world became serene, her heart calm, her mind clear. As Gertrude became more centered, her intention to work from Wholeness grew, but she still didn't know how. *I could operate from a place of appreciation. How would that work?* Having to appreciate Tom made her skin crawl, but she wanted out of the crazy even more.

Heading home from their walk, Gertrude began talking to DB again, "How do I stop myself from reacting to all that I experience at work? How can I hold the vision from the forest, as I work with people who laugh at me on a good day and purposely sabotage me the rest of the time? How do I actually work from Wholeness?"

In silence, they returned home and settled in for the evening, Gertrude reading in bed, DB lying across the bottom, chewing his favorite bone.

Chapter 2

After a bit of time, Gertrude heard a strange voice: "Do you really want to know the answer to all those questions you asked?" She stopped and listened. She had never heard her neighbors before. She lived in a quiet neighborhood. *Where is the voice coming from?* She heard it again, "Do you want to know the answer to all those questions you asked, or were you just venting?"

Gertrude listened once again. *What was going on?*

"Hey, over here. It's me DB . . . Do you really want the answers?"

Gertrude stared at DB in disbelief and with confusion. She had had her share of visions and deep insights, but a talking dog! Come on, this is too weird!

With Gertrude's attention, DB began to answer the questions she had vented earlier that evening.

"Thought is actually a system. One humans don't see. Thought significantly shapes perceptions, your sense of meaning and your daily behavior. Thoughts and knowledge have become so automatic that you are largely controlled by them. With this automation you lose much of your authenticity and freedom. Until you can understand thought more, it can actually control you. You need to be able to perceive your thoughts or you will be under the impression that it responds to your will, that you control your thoughts."

Gertrude was astonished. *What is happening? And yet, it makes sense! How does a dog show such great insight?* She continued to listen to DB.

"This is not conscious. Your thoughts don't realize they are doing this. Mostly you don't want to know. **This unconscious habit is sustained incoherence.**"

"As humans repeat a behavior," DB continued, "it gradually becomes a habit. It just happens over time. This is true with your thoughts also. As it becomes more of a habit you become less and less aware of the thoughts. You assume they are real. How many behaviors do you do automatically to get ready in the morning? You hardly notice how you are doing it. Your thoughts and your feelings do the same thing. This is a big point.

"All these slides in your thinking roll right into your problem solving, but you don't realize this. People assume the problems are out there, somewhere, instead of how you are thinking about the problem." DB paused for a moment.

Gertrude's head was spinning, "So my thinking is the problem?" She was stunned by what was happening.

DB was calm and matter of fact in his response. "Yes, and the incoherence in your system that it creates. Thoughts produce experiences. You are not aware of this happening. We assume it's out there. This awareness and your ability to take responsibility for your thinking and reactions is critical. Assuming everything is 'all out there' is one of your biggest mistakes."

Gertrude took a few deep breaths and started to regain some sense of her sanity. She knew she had better write this down or she would never remember. It seemed really important, but she was not sure what it all meant or how this was happening. *I am thinking the same thoughts over and over and then come to believe they are true. Huh . . . so if they are not reality, how do I stop?*

Gertrude recalled a recent seminar. *This must be what is meant by reality testing in emotional intelligence. How do I learn to increase my reality testing? How do learn to see and interrupt my thoughts? I would have to be able to watch them from a broader view.*

DB lay back down at the end of the bed. He could see she had had enough.

Gertrude stared off into space. She had heard that when the student is ready, the teacher appears, but this?!? Gertrude sat shaking her head, her thoughts whirling. She lay in bed, awake in the dark for a long time before falling asleep.

In the morning, Gertrude was excited and unsettled by the conversation she had with DB last night. She needed to talk. There was one person at Pan Am who she could really trust, Laura, the director of finance. They had been friends for many years, having started on the same day. They had moved up the organization together, survived many meetings and weathered storm after storm after storm. She had heard all of Gertrude's passionate ideas about Wholeness and even read some of the same books. Their lunches where often spent venting about all the crazy or sharing the latest research in leadership and psychological development. It was one of their shared passions.

As an avid student of the works of David Bohm, Laura understood Gertrude's view of the universe, as whole and connected. She too had learned the value of good leadership and experienced the pain of not feeling heard and valued. She knew the importance of listening for essence. Gertrude knew Laura would hear her out and not judge.

Laura was the *only* person Gertrude felt she could tell about the phenomenal events of the last ten days. Would she also mention the talking dog? Or maybe, just wait and see whether Laura could hear DB too? Shaking her head, feeling perplexed, Gertrude was once again reminded of the night before.

Chapter 3

Laura, PanAm's director of finance happened to be on holiday. On her last day, she woke up slowly, just as the birds began to sing their sweet-sounding calls. *Wow, it's been so long since I felt this good. I need to take better care of myself or one day I will wake up on the other side of old.* She lay there, stretching slightly, mindful of some constriction in her body before focusing on her breath and allowing the early morning stillness to sink in. Early dawn was Laura's most favorite part of the day—that moment of stillness and quietude within subtle sounds of nature waking to another day. She knew it was a gift to feel so deeply serene.

For the first time in a long while, Laura's mind was calm. Being an introvert, these past six days on the beach had been heaven. She had been alone for nearly a week, with no one to answer to, taking time for no one else but herself. She had read four books and learned how to paddleboard. It was the perfect blend of water and sun, quiet and fun. She ate really great food, enjoyed a few adult beverages—those ones with the tiny umbrellas—and finally, really slept.

After her long moment of silence, Laura stretched long and slow. It felt so good. She had to remind herself there was no need to hurry. She could take all the time she wanted. It had been quite some time since she had taken vacation; and it was only over the past few days that Laura felt completely relaxed. She took in one more long, deep cleansing breath. Ahhh.

Today was Laura's last day of vacation, and she was going to enjoy every single moment consciously and intentionally. She loved her alone time; but now that she was rested, she missed her friends. She had been texting Gertrude some photos of beautiful sunsets and great meals. After the fifth or sixth text, Gertrude had stopped responding with emojis and started exercising more colorful language. Laura laughed at the game. *Gertrude gets me!*

Laura began thinking about work, which felt natural, given she would be heading home tomorrow. The difference was that she was not in that frenzied place she had been in a week ago. She felt at peace. She felt centered. In balance. *Wow, I have more clarity right now than I have had in a really long time. I have been lost in a blur of overactivity for too long. I love my work, just not my job. I wish there was a way to enjoy it more.*

Laura loved working with numbers; she liked how they all lined up and made sense. She even remembered a time when she loved going to work, but that was becoming a distant memory. At nearly forty years old, she had done well in her career. She also knew she worked too hard, something she had learned from her grandfather. This was her longest vacation in years; and she was so glad she had made the decision to go to the beach, for it was her favorite place . . . her sanctuary. Overall, Laura had great friends and a good life. Yet as Laura's reflections shifted to her actual return to the office, that all too familiar feeling of resistance began to rear its ugly head. She could feel it in the pit of her stomach—that nanosecond of conflict between her head and her heart.

Wait! Is this what I want for my life? Do I really want to settle?

The next day, thoughts began whirling around in Laura's mind as she stared out the window of the 757. Looking out from 36,000 feet, she could feel the tension creeping back in her body. The closer she got to home, the more palpable it became. She closed her eyes, reimagining the beach and the rhythm of ocean waves pounding against the shore. She wasn't going to let her peacefulness slip away. She knew that was real too.

Today was Laura's first day back to the office. She was looking forward to seeing her best friend, Gertrude, to talk about the book on leadership and the new science she had just read. But first, Laura knew she needed to deal with the onslaught. That's the way things were at PanAm—you could take time for yourself only to return to an insurmountable inbox. She took a deep breath and forced a smile, bracing herself as she walked through the door.

Checking in with her direct reports, pouring through nearly 2,000 emails between all the meetings that were scheduled for her, several hours later, Gertrude found Laura buried under a huge pile of work, exhaustion written all over her face. *Poor Laura,* Gertrude thought, *she was having a challenging reentry.*

"Hey Laura," she said, "are you up for dinner tonight? I can't wait to hear about your trip!"

"Yes, absolutely! It's so great to see you!" This was the first bright spot in Laura's workday.

Laura agreed to dinner, even though she still had so much more to do. She preferred a "one and done" approach to completing tasks and in the past would have stayed at the office far after everyone else had left in order to clear her inbox and have a fresh start the next day. But everything would have to wait. This company didn't offer any loyalty and Laura had come to the conclusion that it certainly didn't deserve hers despite the hard work ethic she had learned from her grandfather. She knew this was not the best way to think of her employer, but that's how it was. She also knew dinner with Gertrude would brighten her mood.

Both Laura and Gertrude were single, career women fighting for their place in a very masculine game-playing world. Both knew the support they offered each other was invaluable. It was how they had survived this far.

Gertrude couldn't wait! At 4:55 PM she left her office and met Laura in hers. She could feel Laura's overwhelm. Time to shake it all off! Gertrude knew just the thing. She told her friend about her new fur baby; and with anticipation, Laura followed her home.

As expected, DB greeted them with full doggie excitement. Laura sank to the floor, "Aww, what a great dog! He is so friendly and loving. And super cute! No one could have taken this adorable boy to the shelter." There was just something about DB that brought out delight. After a few minutes of bonding, they all started out on a walk together.

Laura was laughing. "You know someone had a real sense of humor in naming this dog, because David Bohm was a real guy. He was a physicist and wrote a lot about undivided Wholeness, what we now call quantum holographic theory. I am pretty sure I still have one of his books somewhere. He also wrote about how fragmented we all are, which I think is the perfect descriptor for work."

Gertrude let Laura share first; she knew she needed to vent out her day and share about her fabulous vacation. After about forty-five minutes, both women felt more relaxed, enjoying the beautiful evening. They decided to order pizza and opened a bottle of wine.

Now it was Gertrude's moment to begin her fantastic tale. She started by sharing about the vision in the forest and her intention to work from Wholeness and interconnection. Something she now knew was real.

Very present with Gertrude, Laura listened carefully, at times mirroring back what she was hearing. She could see the emotion in Gertrude's eyes, the joy and peace she had felt the night she stumbled upon DB. Laura had had those moments. She could feel it too. *It was a bit like she had felt just two days ago on the beach. Was it only two days ago? Yes, and she wanted more of that.*

Enjoying their wine on the patio, Gertrude was ready to share the weirdest part of all. She began reading the notes she had taken from DB.

After hearing the part where DB spoke, Laura sat up straight, shocked. *What?* She had heard the concepts before, so that was all good. But a talking dog?!? Laura had absolutely no way to wrap her head around this.

The idea of a talking dog was crazy! He was sitting right here. They had gone for a walk together. That had all been good. He had looked and acted completely normal.

At least the ideas that DB had shared were things she understood. From her training on learning organizations, Laura knew that "mental models" were ways of thinking that limited clear perception. What she remembered from the seminar about what it meant to *suspend* and *allow* until she could understand better. Maybe she could do that *for now*.

Laura calmed herself; she knew Gertrude was not psychotic. And DB was not talking now.

Laura liked Gertrude's intention to work from Wholeness and interconnection. She really needed this. She was all in! Both women were excited to start this journey together. It would be great to have a companion and really commit to help each other hold a clear vision in spite of all that they saw and felt at work.

"Let's start on Friday for breakfast," Laura said, excited to begin. "That will give me a couple of days to catch up. And we will really need to fortify our resolve before the dreaded leadership meeting. It will be our biggest challenge. We probably need to make Friday breakfast a regular thing."

"Absolutely," Gertrude said. "We can come up with our game plan on what to do when the shit flies. Without a clear plan, I don't see how we will remember when things get chaotic. So, our first task on Friday is to decide how we handle the toxic atmosphere of the meetings. How hard can that be?" She began laughing.

"That sounds like a great plan! What could possibly go wrong?" Laura said, laughing in unison with Gertrude. "Let's keep it simple; small steps that we can keep doing. We need to clarify our intention too; make things as concrete as possible, so when we both lose it, we can remember why we are doing this. Oh, and our first rule: only one of us can lose it at a time!"

Laura laughed again, as she walked out the door to head home, feeling once again connected and hopeful.

Gertrude felt the same way, as she started dancing around the living room with DB in her arms.

"I now have a plan and a partner! I have a way to step out of the crazy madness. I don't know how long it will take, but we have started the journey, DB! We have started!"

DB wagged his tail and licked Gertrude's face in agreement.

Chapter 4

Laura and Gertrude agreed to meet twice a week to strengthen their intention, share their learnings, and most importantly, figure out how to create a new way of being within the lunacy of PanAm. Together they would define and hold a clear vision to shift out of the toxicity and fragmentation of the organization and bring peace and coherence into their daily work.

As the week went by, Gertrude found herself still getting caught in her old anger and thoughts, especially when Tom went on his latest rampage. She was caught in a no-woman's land. She knew her negative thoughts really needed to shift, but they came so automatically. And they absolutely felt like the truth. *Wow, my negative thoughts are part of the toxicity! I didn't realize I was holding on to these judgments about Tom. They come so quickly. And despite how right these thoughts feel to me, this is not what is going to get me out of the crazy. What do I want more? Being right? Or expanding into Wholeness? I can see so many other ways to view what is happening if I can suspend my old beliefs. If I keep my anger, I feel powerful for a while, righteous even. But I am stuck in my own shit. I guess it is about choosing, refocusing my attention moment to moment; and then doing it again and again. Whew! Okay, right now,*

withdraw my attention into this moment and breathe, small consistent steps! Gertrude reminded herself.

Gertrude was looking forward to her first meeting with Laura, her mind filled with questions. *How can we remember Wholeness in all the anger? What does a strategy of peace look like? Oh God, we will have to stop the griping about the others all the time, not just in the meetings. Wow, that will be hard! It's so much easier to complain.* There was so much to think about.

Friday breakfast finally came. The first step would be about interrupting their judgmental thoughts about Tom.

- ❖ Withdrawing, refocusing, and reframing their attention.
- ❖ Stopping the verbal and mental complaining.

Both agreed they would hold their attention on these two practices as a way to start; they need to become new habits, a new reflex. If Gertrude and Laura focus only on the toxicity, they will never begin. They need to start where they are.

At the conclusion of the breakfast, Laura suggested, "Tuesday morning, let's begin to outline what we know; what we have read; and what we have learned so far. We have actually been reading and discussing all of this for quite some time, already. So, let's gather that data and build from there. Then we can figure out how we can help each other to refocus our attention better. Oh yeah and stop all the negative thoughts about Tom."

Gertrude laughed, "Sure, let's start small."

The leadership meeting came and went. Both women held strong and didn't enter into the fray. That's not to say they didn't think really loud, nasty thoughts! The anger, resentment, and frustration still filled them. At least *they* had begun to see the polluted, contaminated system they called PanAm. "Okay, so I think we did pretty well for our first try," Laura said as they walked to their cars later that day. "Just keeping our mouths shut was a total win!"

"Yeah," Gertrude agreed, "this condescension and purposely embarrassing people is completely the norm; and I really wanted to jump in. Now that I can see it more clearly, it's actually worse than I realized. Reality testing is not always fun. We have a long way to go. But I am totally counting it as a win! Do you want to have dinner? I have food and DB needs his walk. We can finish writing out our intention. It's pretty hard to remember all of this when the shit is flying; I want to have an outline in front of me in those meetings."

"Sure," Laura said, "that sounds great. I need to get gas and run a few errands; so, I will meet you in a few."

Laura checked out DB, while they were walking; still just a normal dog, nothing unusual here.

After walking DB and a bit of cooking, the women settled in with Mexican food on the outside patio.

Gertrude relaxed, "There have been a lot of good moments this week. I am not nearly as exhausted. Hope sure brings out some good endorphins."

"Absolutely!" Laura chimed in. "Even in the leadership meeting I was able to observe the toxicity. It felt less personal. I felt more like a fly on the wall than a combatant." Laura stretched out and let out a sigh. Life was good. A sense of tranquillity returned and expanded, sounds of nature filling the moment.

"So, tell me again," Laura asked, "what you felt when you knew you could work from Wholeness. What does that mean to you? What does it look like?"

Gertrude took a deep breath, "It's such a big idea. For me it means deep interconnection, knowing at some level we are all one. I see Wholeness as the deep connection of all living things, operating beneath our current belief of separation. I remember a quote something like: A world where the unseen is the primary influencer, where smaller is most powerful. For me, the quantum holographic Whole is where Wholeness becomes primary, who I am and how I show up matters. My thoughts, actions and intentions feed the field. I choose the Field of Love. For me it's an actual energetic field.

"I remember reading some of Teilhard de Chardin's work. He talked about Love as a force of nature, fulfilling the physics definition of work. He argued that Love is the most powerful and pervasive source of energy in the world—not gravity, electromagnetism, or the nuclear forces. Love is a field that fills and enfolds us, a field of interconnection.

"Science has readily accepted the idea of interconnection but are still learning about and discovering its reality. We get to work from this view right now! Even where there is toxicity, it is happening within Wholeness. We are shifting our viewpoint to the Whole, pulling our attention away from all the toxicity. It's big work! And we need to do it, even if we are stumbling along.

"I am so happy we are doing this together. I know we've had so many conversations about these ideas. It is really just putting it all together in a practical way. It's OK that it takes us some time and we fumble around. It's all good, as least we are not unconscious."

"Hey," Laura interjected, "as you were sharing, I remembered something . . . What we choose, with each action and thought, is an intention, a quality of consciousness that we bring to the situation. So, we are intentionally choosing the quality of our consciousness, our mental, emotional and physical states, and the direction toward which we turn our attention. It's more than simply holding an intention;

it's continuously and consciously choosing who we are and how we will act."

"So, the intention," Gertrude continued, "would be something about working from Wholeness, or even working from Love—capital L Love. We remember it as we go about our day, regardless of what we see out there. And we help each other remember; we check in. We stay centered in our heart, mind and body. I know there are some great grounding programs on the meditation timer I use. I will bookmark those so I can get there quick and stay in my body and not run in my mind when I am upset.

"I would say **our intention is to remember Wholeness and to remember Love is real** as we walk about our day making all the small adjustments in our thoughts and behaviors that we need to do to stay aligned. As we do this, we can both move out of fragmentation into physical coherence. That is definitely the first step, that and not feeding the spinning thoughts. We bring all aspects of our self into alignment; and together, synchronize with Undivided Wholeness.

"Yay! That's good!" Gertrude clapped her hands.

"So, as the first draft of our intention: **Align with Wholeness/Love. Do our work; surrender our reactions; be present to see opportunities to align deeper; and let go of the outcome. This is where we really have to trust in Wholeness.** If we end up leaving this job, finding a better place, I am okay with that. Letting all of the toxicity go is critical, however it happens. What do you think? What would you add or change, Laura?"

Laura reflected. "What we have so far feels right. I know we have read enough leadership literature to know that all of this includes things like strong emotional intelligence and operating in a way that is aligned with our values."

"Yeah," Gertrude interrupted. "I don't object to the stated values of Pan Am—it's the way they ignore them. It's almost funny how integrity is one of the stated values, yet most of us here are completely out of integrity. And this shows up every single day!" She laughed, continuing, "Our newly stated intention helps us improve our lives and those around us. Our departments will certainly benefit. Who knows, maybe even beyond that? Right now, I can't see how the organization would buy in; but that is part of what we surrender. We clearly don't have control over anything but us. We never have, so giving up the delusion is good. We do our work, internally and externally; and we look for opportunities to know Wholeness more deeply."

"In business terms, we can refer to our value-based practices as emotional intelligence and clear critical thinking when we decide to share it with anybody. It's both of those things.

So, this intention puts us back into integrity," Laura responded, then added. "I like the alignment of our behavior and values. It feels strong. It makes us each accountable for our own thoughts and behaviors. No playing the victim. We are out of the blame game; that alone is a huge energy suck.

"I like using the word Love, so I'll stay with that," Laura declared. "We know we mean the same thing."

"Yes," Gertrude jumped in, "and I will stay with Wholeness. We don't need to be carbon copies of each other, just support each other where we are.

"Wow, this has been intense. Let's go walk DB again. He has been so good out here with us; time for some doggie loving. And he's definitely part of Wholeness too!"

DB jumped up at the word walk, tail wagging, ready to go!

"Hey, DB did you hear our intention is getting stronger? What do you think?" Gertrude asked.

DB's eye's sparkled but didn't say a word. Apparently, he only talks on his terms.

The following Tuesday morning, Laura shared about a book she had read on the beach. Ahh, just the memory of it took her back to the smell of the salt air and sound of the pounding waves. *"The author talked about organizational fields that interconnect groups of people."* Laura shared from the book, "Margaret Wheatley defines these fields as unseen energy stating that an organization is a field, an interconnection of people, thoughts, choices, problems, and solutions, flowing around, creating a field of energy. She states that these fields can influence our behavior, cohering, and organizing events."

"That makes so much sense! How else could such unproductive behavior appear normal?" Gertrude commented, "this fits perfectly with what we talked about. It sounds like as we shift our state of being, we help hold a new field dynamic—first in our own mental/emotional state and then, as both of us get more coherent, we influence the group."

Laura continued sharing from Wheatley's book, "The more present and aware we are as individuals and as organizations, the more choices we create. As awareness increases, we can engage with more possibilities. We are no longer held prisoner by habits, unexamined thoughts, or information at which we refuse to look.

"Every act of observation loses more information than it gains. Whatever we decide to notice blinds us to other possibilities.

In directing our attention to certain things, we lose awareness of everything else. We collapse the world of possibilities into a narrow band of observation."

"That sounds exactly like our first step," Gertrude exclaimed. "Shifting our attention away from the toxicity, redirecting it to Undivided Wholeness! Oops, look at the time; we better go."

Gertrude and Laura's conversation ended abruptly, as work impinged on their peaceful reverie; but their resolve and their intention were gaining strength. Both women left with smiling faces and a sense of delight.

Later that day, as Gertrude drove home, she reflected upon all the ideas she and Laura discussed. This process of discovery was becoming very exciting, but what about that conversation with DB? *Did my dog really talk to me? Maybe it was a dream. Nonetheless, it's had such an impact already.*

Chapter 5

The day had finally arrived for Gertrude and Laura to begin the meditation class in the park. It was a perfect way to just *be*. Her talks with Laura and her walks with DB made Gertrude feel healthier, and her work felt lighter. She knew nothing had changed, except, of course, her perception, which was really helping. As long as she could remember that Wholeness always includes other ways to see, she could suspend her locked-in thoughts/beliefs. The stress and dread she was accustomed to feeling every morning was almost gone. Her ideas were more creative, her thoughts more fluid. Even her staff had begun to notice.

The shift in her department was unexpected. Of course it made sense; she was just a bit surprised. She was listening better to her people; her mood calmer; and the work was more cohesive. Her employees were expressing their creativity and laughing more. The tension was definitely down. This was happening within Finance too, putting a small bubble of harmony around the women and their departments. The confidence and clarity were powerful.

Gertrude continued her walks in the forest with DB, occasionally venting. The forest itself is so calming. It all felt so much better. She didn't care if it started with a talking dog. There were still problems; but as she turned inward, her deep sense of calm grew stronger and stronger each day. Gertrude felt the light each time she walked in the forest. The field of Love continued to surround her and DB. It seemed to be getting stronger the more she chose to work from Wholeness.

Gertrude smiled as she watched DB. He was pure joy. He would prance down the trail, sniffing with enthusiasm. Every once in a while, a small stream of golden light shimmered from him. Gertrude noticed this was beginning to happen with the trees too. The light was adding rays of color to almost everything around her.

Late one evening, after one of their walks, Gertrude heard the voice once again. "It looks like you and Laura are doing well with understanding how your perceptions are an extension of your thoughts, observing and releasing your assumptions. So, let's talk some more about this."

Wide-eyed, Gertrude stared at DB, as he continued, "Thought operates as a system. This human system includes thoughts, feelings, even the state of the body and society as a whole. Thoughts are passed back and forth between you, and this exchange has been evolving since ancient times. And this system has a fault in it. It's not just here or there, it is throughout the whole system. It is basic conditioning, the repetition of which leaves a mark on our nervous system. Your physiology is altered. As you can see, this has been present throughout all the problems of the world, working by a set of reflexes. To deal with this, people use the fragmentary thought that produced the problem. This is what Einstein meant when he said you can't solve a problem with the same level of thinking that created it. Fragmented thought creates fragmented solutions."

Gertrude, who had been reading in bed, was sitting straight up now, a cold shiver running down her back, "Hold on. Are you saying our thoughts actually change our bodies? That even when I am sure I am thinking clearly I may not be! No way! I get that I have a habit of thinking certain thoughts; and I need to learn to suspend them so I can be more

A Call to Wholeness

creative and allow better solutions to emerge. That is the essence of the creative process, after all. But have I actually been changing my body by repeating the same thoughts over and over, and then holding on to the error in my thinking!?! I have been doing this for years!"

"Yes," DB continued. "And it is all done without your awareness. These conditioned reflexes affect feelings and then trigger chemical reactions in the body, affecting your thinking. It becomes a chain reaction, one thought leading to another. You think you are in control of your thoughts, creating your thoughts, but they are automatic. Most of human thinking is a reflex. So, everything we call thought is a system of reflexes."

Gertrude was shaking her head. "Chain reactions of thoughts... is that why it's so hard in the meetings? My reflexes get triggered, and I don't even realize it. I have patterns in my nervous system holding them in place." She had heard a lot of talk about "rewiring" her brain, but she didn't realize it was so literal. "Wow! This is all so overwhelming and yet makes perfect sense."

Gertrude looked at DB, amazed but not surprised.

DB continued, "These reflexes can serve you but don't if you are too rigid. They don't work if your minds are jumping all around. Remember, you are breaking an old mold of thought. From here, you can shift into a new thought."

Gertrude interrupted, as she was now writing furiously in the notebook she kept on the side table, "So, when we can shift our physical state to coherence—to more clear and calm states—we can begin to watch our thoughts and choose different ones?"

"Yes!" DB said. But Gertrude wasn't listening. DB stopped talking and laid back down. He watched Gertrude lost in her notes.

"This makes sense; it's practical and something we can do." Gertrude knew this is what she had experienced in the forest—a flash of insight, something beyond words. When she was in the forest, she had been so upset, there was no choice but to let everything go. Then the light filled her; and she knew Wholeness without any words to describe it. Her body relaxed; her breathing settled. She had slipped into a coherent state without even knowing what it was.

Letting go of expectations and locked down beliefs appears to be a key to expanding perception. Then we just need the "muscle" to pull ourselves out of our reflexes. She had expected the world to be toxic and fragmented; so, she had kept seeing it that way.

Gertrude tried to process all this out loud. "Thought was a system with a fault in it. We have to learn to observe, to step back and see what we are really thinking and if we are really just reacting out of habit." That was true of every corporate job Gertrude had ever had. The toxicity, the habit and belief in passive-aggressive behavior... "Wow! No wonder it all seemed so real! We think a thought, and the body creates the matching feeling. So, to really see, we must break through the way we have conditioned our bodies to respond! Both David Bohm's work and cognitive-behavioral therapy suggests our capacity for clear critical thinking significantly affects our worldview—our capacity to see problems clearly and to solve them. But this capacity rests in our physical state. Because perception follows thought. We will see what we think about. Actually, we will look for what we think about, then call anything that is close, true. Confirmation bias at its finest! These reflexes are also biochemical; so, they affect the body and our feelings. So, crazy, fragmented states prevent clarity.

"Wait!" Gertrude exclaimed. "This is like what I learned in design school—to work from an expanded field of possibilities and allow a new vision to emerge into my artwork. This is the process of creativity!

"The next step would be to manage the reflexes and then to somehow watch and adjust our thoughts to expand our capacity. Also, to remember that every thought we think is not real, just because we think it is. Ahh . . . this is where the silence practice comes in. This is where I feel the vastness."

Gertrude remembered hearing about a concept called a *meme*, where repetition of an idea makes it "true." *This must be what happens with our thoughts: We culturally decide what something means and repeat it until it becomes truth. This is actually the habit we need to step back from personally, in teams, in companies, and within the entire human system*, Gertrude thought as she went to sleep, once again with her head spinning.

Chapter 6

The next morning, Gertrude remembered she had read about some techniques that worked to reset the nervous system and help balance the chemical responses of the body. This seemed to be exactly what was needed; she couldn't wait to talk to Laura.

At Friday's breakfast, both women were full of excitement and information they had learned over the last few days. Gertrude shared with Laura what DB had said. "Our thoughts are a system that works as a set of reflexes. It's a form of conditioning and repeating something quite often leaves a mark in our bodies. This reflex is part of the crazy behavior at PanAm. It is unconscious and goes against all the organization's stated values."

"Hey Gertrude," said Laura, "look what I found in one of my yoga books this weekend. It's a yoga sutra, one of the rules of practice. 'Yoga is the suppression of the oscillations of the mental substance.' This is thousands of years old, and it is saying the same thing!"

Gertrude jumped in, "Wow, we are going to need to really balance our physical state to help make this easier. I can feel all those stress chemicals churning through me when Tom speaks. Actually, they stay around all the time I am at work. I am better at home. My walks with DB are so helpful. I look at him, and I go into Love, and I can remember Wholeness so much easier!"

"How do we actually be calm and kind?" Laura wondered aloud.

Gertrude replied, "I don't like being in that churned up state, either. I want to really remember Love and Wholeness when we are in those meetings. Do you remember when we learned about HeartMath?"

"No, I don't think so," Laura said.

"It was at our last leadership training," Gertrude continued. "I looked it up after we got back and sent it to you. It's a system that teaches us how to calm ourselves down and bring ourselves back into balance physically and emotionally. We focus on our breath in a specific way to consciously move ourselves into coherence. Coherence is a physical state that synchronizes our heart, lung, and autonomic nervous system. So, the systems in our body all start working together. It helps balance our feelings, teaching us a way to override all those stress chemicals from our emotional reflexes. I think it will help us integrate our mental capacities with our heart. Anyway, I think we need to learn this system."

Laura now remembered reading some information about emotional refocusing and restructuring techniques. Now she knew what that really meant and how it could help. Both women agreed to find out where they could learn more. It seemed like the best way to break the patterns of limiting thoughts that were running amuck in their minds. They could check into this after they finished the meditation class. They really needed something they could do on demand, like walking down the hall at work!

Gertrude mused, "With this shift into coherence and suspending our thoughts, we really have a powerful combination. This is the state a value-based leader ideally leads from. Without being clear and calm, it's too easy to get lost in our reactions. The reality is, we can't know everything; so we need to suspend. We stay calm and we allow. This runs counter to current business culture. Yet, pretending we actually know is a delusion. Reality testing again requires us to accept what we don't know and allow the solution to emerge. Because in Wholeness the solution already exists! Separation isn't real. To seek to know the unknown is foundational to both science and even the mystical level of most religions. To know the unknown, we are by definition, working from the assumption that we aren't perfect. It's what creates the vacuum, the space for novel ideas and shifts in our behavior to emerge."

"You know, Gertrude," Laura said sarcastically, "this alone would reduce our meetings to pure panic. I don't know anyone in the meeting that would be willing to admit they don't know something!"

Gertrude and Laura were so happy that they didn't have to clear away all their limiting beliefs, prejudices, or anger before they began. The only thing required of them was to be aware and accept where they were, allowing their thoughts and feelings, noticing their reactions, and then simply shifting their attention every time they become aware of having feelings. This new habit would really help in the meetings.

Gertrude interjected, "I really like our meditation class. As we turn inward and notice our spinning minds, we know we have not moved deeply enough into Wholeness, as it expands us into our highest, true selves. Our own awareness—our interiority—runs much deeper than we realize, as it is connected to Wholeness, to Source. A contemplative practice is the best practical way to rewire our minds and move deeper into our hearts. Just like exercise, it the best long-term practice for overall well-being. The silence from our practice dips into the unconscious, healing us at depth, where all our hidden wounds and anger lie. It is in this silence where transformation occurs."

After only two months, so many things were already falling into place. The women were more peaceful and had learned so much. Things were becoming clearer and they could see a bigger picture—even how the leadership trainings they attended over the past several years integrated into the intention they set and the practices they have begun. And, of course, there were also the lessons from DB.

So much of business is tied to ideas that are hundreds of years out of date. The traditional business model is all about power, politics, greed, command, and control and the ends justifying the means. Niccolò Machiavelli wrote about this in the 1500s. Yes, 500 years ago. It's laughable how old this approach is and yet how it is still the primary way business operates—even fifty years after the introduction of value-based leadership! Culture holds memory. The old system has such a strong grip on us that it operates nearly invisibly.

Gertrude was in her office when she heard a ruckus. Normally she would stay away, but today she felt a strong pull. A crowd was gathering. Tom, his face blood red, was screaming at Laura, going off, calling her a f*cking bitch in the middle of the lobby. Laura took a deep breath, using all of her capacity to be professional in this very public area. The yelling of expletives was not new behavior from Tom, but she had never before been his direct target.

Taking a deeper breath and looking Tom straight in the eye, in a clear and strong voice, Laura said, "Tom, your behavior is not appropriate. Over and above the fact that people should never be treated this way, this is a workplace requiring professional behavior. I don't appreciate you speaking to me in this manner and tone. If you expect me to work with you, your behavior must change. And let's be clear, you need me to work with you." Laura then turned and walked back to her office. Tom continued to yell as she walked away.

Gertrude arrived just as Laura was addressing Tom. To her, she looked accomplished, composed, and strong. Gertrude turned around and went to Laura's office through the back hall. She caught the closing door and stepped in behind Laura. "Time to figure out what the hell just happened! Now is the time to use our intention as the tool it is."

Gertrude led Laura through the process they had created so far. "Okay, let's start with some silence and our breath work," she began. "We can use our HeartMath coherence techniques during this whole discussion. Here are our working questions: 'What is my state? How do I act from Wholeness here? What is the quality of my consciousness?'"

The ladies worked it through. The deep knowing of interconnection supported by their willingness to let it all go. But not without some venting and realigning. This had been an extremely upsetting moment for Laura—to be made a target in front of so many other people, with Tom relentlessly screaming at her. On the outside, she may have appeared poised. On the inside, she was shaking and felt sick to her stomach. The incident reminded her of her childhood, with her father's angry outbursts and her striving for perfection as a coping mechanism to stop all the yelling. Laura had come a long way over the years, but this moment in the lobby took her back, poking old inner demons. With Gertrude's help, the women got themselves all the way down to mental, emotional, and physical peace.

"Okay, I feel a lot better," Laura said, feeling somewhat renewed. "Thanks for your help. I have more clarity and I am ready to do some strategizing!"

In the end, the women agreed to give Tom as little of their attention as possible. They would withdraw attention from the toxicity. Ultimately, they agreed Laura would file a formal complaint with HR. Working from Wholeness didn't include being a doormat. This behavior existed as part of the reality of Pan Am and needed to be addressed.

As always, the incident was jarring for both of them. It was a total drain on their energy and attention. But this time was also different as they were able to shift mentally, emotionally, and physically within an hour. The clarity changed their response and strengthened their point with HR. They had made the commitment and this incident was exactly why. Their resolve moved deeper. They felt stronger. Aligned. The momentum was building, and momentum is the gold in any business.

Their women's Tuesday meetings continued to focus on leadership literature. Laura had been reading more about fields and their dynamics. Tom's repeated, tolerated behavior fit this exactly. From a book in her hands, she read, "The field of a business is created by repetition—the totality of all the thoughts, choices, and actions of its members—over and over again. The awareness of this can change the environment—the culture of an organization—in a sustainable way." She paused, then surmised, "So, if the repetition of yelling and screaming can create a field, then it seems reasonable that the repetition of respect and mindful action can also impact the field. If we can reset and 'rewire' our autonomic nervous system, it stands to reason we can reset this culture."

"Yes, I know we just started and this culture has been locked down in toxicity for years, but I can already feel a tiny change," Gertrude agreed.

Laura continued reading. "The shift comes from understanding the reality of our interconnection. When we use force, we create equal and opposite reactions. Shifting our attention to Wholeness is the point of transformation. It is Wholeness that transforms leaders and organizations. There is a sense of 'knowingness,' a sense of connected wisdom, confidence, and clarity of action. There is Love."

"Wow," Gertrude exclaimed, "this is saying the same thing! Culture as a key to success. It's a much more expanded view. How many times have we heard that similar Peter Drucker quote, 'Culture eats strategy for breakfast'?

"Many," Laura said, adding, "this is taking all we have learned in our value-based leadership training and moving it deeper into the new science. We know that grounding ourselves physically dramatically improves our critical thinking. And from this clarity, we can choose who we are and how we show up. This becomes the basis for the new field—a new holding environment. How did people even think of leading without these capacities?"

Laura loved how this was all coming together. There was definitely synchronicity going on here. "Who knew that the answer was here all along? We only needed the willingness to see."

She continued, "The new science suggests leadership operates as a frequency, an attractor pattern. It's like how my phone picks up my number and not yours. Both are frequencies. It's in phase lock—a pattern match at an energetic level. Leadership, just like everything else, is energy.

"The new science recognizes a field as an energy dynamic. Think about why we have been so careful to not let anyone else in on what we are doing. We are shifting our own state first. If we share our ideas too soon, the dominant field will take us over.

"This pattern organizes space-time. Systems are bigger than people. It is like there is an unconscious set of rules. And here at PanAm, yelling at each other and dropping F-bombs is acceptable. You don't have to have a Ph.D. to know that's bad for business. Yet it keeps happening. Everyone is just pretending there is no other choice. We are so lucky to have stepped out of the toxic craziness—to be working out of conscious choice and to decide how we show up."

"Yeah," Gertrude sighed, "it's been tough; it's taken real strength and discipline. But it so worth it!"

"Yes, absolutely!" Laura agreed. "You know we aren't the only ones here who have been to the leadership trainings. The leadership team knows the basics of value-based leadership. No one uses it, but they have learned it."

The women had developed a rhythm where they are now able to interrupt their negative spirals quicker and quicker. Both were sleeping deeper and had so much more energy. With the beautiful fall weather, they had taken to speed walking in the evenings. DB was a big fan of this new routine.

"Well, clearly work is still a shit show, but wow, I do feel better overall!" Laura exclaimed. This was all so exciting. Since they had agreed to work in this new way, the flood gates had opened. So many things were connecting, the synchronicity building. Even after they found out Tom got a new car for "having" to go to anger management classes; so typical in business. Both ladies knew their intention was bigger than Tom. And that is what they focused on.

Chapter 7

A few hours after their Friday breakfast meeting, both women were sitting with the leadership team. From the outside, everything looked the same. For the ladies, the meetings had become like a big game. This one was a test of their capacity to hold steady, and they were ready.

The undertone of anger and hostility was gone from both Gertrude and Laura. What they had found in this process was bigger than the organization or its flaws. Both were genuinely interested in doing their best and supporting the entire company. Even when the shots came and the nastiness filled the room, both Gertrude and Laura stayed true to their intention and breathed deeply. This process was getting easier with more practice. The ladies had begun sitting across from each other to help anchor and support their intention, strengthened by the direct eye contact they were now able to make across the boardroom table. The change in their seats and their responses was beginning to get noticed by some of the other directors.

Both Gertrude and Laura continued to be silent about their intention. Like the misogynist he was, Tom made a comment about how they were "finally behaving." *Oops, that was a slip! Back to coherence,* Gertrude thought with a laugh.

Wait, can I realize he is misogynist and stay in coherence? This is interesting; staying in coherence doesn't change the sexism. It changes my reaction and attachment to it. This is that witness/observer piece taught in meditation. It actually gives me a clear calm platform for giving voice to the issue. Definitely something I need to keep building toward. Eventually, we will both need to be clear and calm and able to stand up against toxicity, dominance, and discrimination.

In the hall, after the leadership meeting, Bob, a senior vice-president, came up to Gertrude and Laura, complementing them on their positive participation in the meeting. Gertrude and Laura both smiled and thanked him, as they walked away.

In Laura's office, they broke into a happy dance.

As time flew by, positive results of their coherence practice continued to build. There were plenty of opportunities to shift their state and consciously focus on Wholeness. At times, the ladies both fell into the nonsense, but it didn't last. As soon as they remembered their intention, it helped to pull each other out of negativity. Those old biochemical reflexes where still there, but Laura and Gertrude refused to get stuck again. They continued to allow themselves to learn in their own space and time, and their optimism was becoming obvious—infectious even.

Gertrude and Laura were sitting out on the patio after another successful week, laughing and drinking wine. DB was happily sitting at their feet, watching for squirrels "I can't believe it has only been a few months!" Laura practically screamed. "On my way back from vacation, I was almost in tears at the thought of coming back. Now, I actually enjoy my job most of the time. It seems almost too simple. Do you remember our original plan? Mostly, we wanted to survive the dread of going to work and those horrible Friday leadership meetings!"

Gertrude agreed. "I can't believe the shift. I laugh so much more! I feel like we are so lucky; and yet I know we chose this and have been working hard to get here. I am pretty proud of us. We are doing it! And you know, Bob has really noticed. He likes it, but I don't think he gets it. Should we start talking about it?"

In silence, Laura reflected for a long moment. Then she said, "I have been thinking. You know how when I plant my herbs every year, I have to harden-off the seedlings before I put them in the ground? They have to get use to the wind and the rain. They aren't as strong or don't survive as well if they are planted too soon. How do we do that here? How do we 'harden off' this process? Is there a way we can begin to introduce these ideas, little by little?

"I like our bubble," Laura continued. "I love how my intuition is so much stronger. It's like I can think more clearly. So yes, I want to do this; and I don't want to. Does that make sense?"

"Yes," Gertrude said." I get it. I don't want it to blow up. I love the peace and my silence in the morning, and there's a part of me that doesn't want to disrupt that."

With that, the ladies allowed for silence.

DB broke the quiet, and said, "You are really getting the shift necessary to move out of the crazy fragmentation and into coherence. I am so proud of you!"

Laura was so startled by the talking animal that she jumped and spilled her drink. Gertrude started laughing so hard that tears ran down her face. The fish look on Laura's face was classic! After Gertrude wiped away the tears, she said, "See, Laura, it really is true! I have a talking dog."

Laura remained speechless.

DB continued, "As you have seen when we can suspend carrying out our impulses, suspend believing our assumptions, and look at them, then we are all in the same state of consciousness. When we are in a group with a defensive attitude, blocking and holding assumptions, sticking to them, and saying, 'I have got to be right,' then intelligence is very limited. Carrying this clarity and openness into a group discussion allows for Dialogue. That's Dialogue with a capital D."

"Dialogue with a capital D?" Laura and Gertrude asked at the same time. "So that's how we can begin to bring this to the group? Through Dialogue?"

"I have heard of Dialogue," Laura said. "It's when a group slows down and really listens without judgment as a way to fully understand one another. It is from this place that all possibility is born because it's where Love and acceptance become known and practiced. But how would we ever do this at PanAm?"

DB replied, "Dialogue extends and expands that sense of coherence you have each felt internally into the group. It allows for differences and conflicting views to be voiced and actively listened to. Just like you have learned to hold steady individually, Dialogue allows the group to come into balance and hold the dynamics at a higher level of functioning. So, you ladies, in a way, have already started to introduce this."

Laura interrupted, "So you are saying that when Gertrude and I hold clear and calm in the leadership meetings, we are already moving toward Dialogue. Oh wait ... of course, because of how we show up, we are holding the environment."

"Right!" DB explained. "When you are in conversation, often times you will discover that you have a different sentiment, observation, opinion, or idea and, because of that, the exchange becomes heated—sometimes even toxic! These types of conversations conclude with either a frustrating stalemate or the competitive sense that there are winners and losers. Or maybe even a rampage. In short, Dialogue is about seeking mutual understanding and harmony through seeing all others as legitimate. That's why I label it with a capital D."

"Well, mutual understanding is a long way from our leadership meetings," Gertrude jumped in. "It's taken us months to be able to be neutral in that environment, and we do that for our peace of mind, not Tom's. Help me see how I would shift to see him as legitimate."

"I understand. As human beings, you are prone to attachment," DB empathized. "What I mean by this is that you experience your assumptions, beliefs, opinions, and ideas as truth, making you right and others wrong. Then when someone disagrees or challenges the truth with which you identify, you feel attacked and your emotions become engaged. This is typically when you will start to defend your views, because you feel them as though they are an inseparable part of you. A challenge to your emotions is therefore an implied threat to your wellbeing. This is why so many conversations end unproductively and discussions aimed at healing rifts so often deepen them."

"So really," Gertrude clarified, "we are just holding on to our old beliefs and keep reinforcing them with every interaction with Tom. Using our new practices, and in responding to Tom differently, we have sort of locked in a new way of being. I know you are not saying everything is okay with Tom's behavior. We have to focus on shifting first within ourselves and then hold the space for the environment to shift. Okay, Laura, I guess it really is time to take our new way of being into the organization."

There was a long silence. DB settled back down like nothing had happened.

Gertrude thought about all that was said. *Dialogue . . . capital D. Listening . . . understanding . . . acceptance and being accessible to everyone. Hmm . . . it seems like a great idea.*

She finally broke the quiet. "I am not confused by the reality of the toxic culture. Step by step and hold steady; that is how we have come this far and how we will bring this to the larger organization."

"We need to find a way to meet people where they are," Laura chimed in. "If we start too far over the threshold, we will get immediate resistance. We have been reading and talking about these ideas and concepts for a very long time. And we are part of a very small group who actively pays attention in the leadership seminars, she added with a smirk. "We need to remember that other people in the organization have had less experience with this kind of stuff. And let's face it, we've been in our own little secret bubble, practicing and experimenting, learning and applying. Oh yeah, let's not forget the biggest secret of all—our talking dog! And then there's Tom; he will be our biggest resister! And I'm thinking about that incident in the lobby, which could add possible fuel to fire. We will need some anchors. And some champions. Who do you think could be our best supporters? Who are our allies?"

"I am not completely sure," Gertrude said. "What if we start looking for openings and let Wholeness bring us to the best solutions? We simply allow Wholeness and Love. We don't want to resist; that's out of coherence. So, we slow down and allow and respond to the opportunities."

"I'm in," Laura stated. "But I want to be really careful. I'm not willing to be continuously bashed upside the head, but these practices could help the team so much. And that is what feels so meaningful to me. I'm willing to take the risk for something greater."

"Oh good, sounds like a plan." Gertrude picked up DB's squeaky ball and threw it out into the yard. DB ran happily after it. *Is this the same dog that was talking just a few moments ago?* she wondered.

Laura and Gertrude continued cheerfully along, more aware of how their internal shifts were affecting the group. They had learned to sit in silence each morning and use the mindfulness techniques they learned from the HeartMath Institute, practicing them throughout the day. They even began playing with and watching the effects of Dialogue in the meetings, integrating the tenets of values-based leadership.

Both had more energy and joy. Their coherent state made letting go of the negativity so much easier. It seemed that the uncontrollable was becoming controllable by being more aware and stabilizing their internal state. And having a partner to help was huge!

Chapter 8

Bob was stopping the ladies regularly now to talk. He kept asking questions. Gertrude and Laura decided they would bring Bob into their bubble when the opportunity presented itself. They would start small and speak in only business/scientific terms. No talking dog required!

Robert (Bob) Turner had been a SVP of PanAm for five years. His stress level was off the charts, and he had the blood pressure and cholesterol to prove it. His doctor had asked him to up his meds, but he rarely remembered to take the ones he had. By the time he left work, he was so tired, he didn't care what he ate or if he exercised. "Just give me a beer."

Since his divorce two years ago, Bob could do what he wanted. So, he worked hard and left it all at the office. He was burned out; he had no life. For the most part he saw his department heads do the same. Their message was, "Broadcasting is an intense business, so man up!"

Bob had deeper demons than most. And it's not that Bob didn't want to fight the good fight; he would if he felt he had a plan, a way. Bob knew that something was missing in his life and work; things didn't feel as meaningful as they did in earlier days. He just felt so lost. He had pushed his vision away, and it made him feel powerless.

Bob knew something was shifting, however. It seemed to be centered with Gertrude and Laura. It started about the time Laura came back from vacation four months ago. The third quarter numbers where clear. He could see the decrease in opposition and the increase in productivity around creative services and finance. This kind of decrease in conflict, especially about money, didn't just happen on its own. Something was up. But he didn't know what.

He was getting the accolades from his boss, but he knew he wasn't doing anything. At some point, the CEO was going to want to know what was happening. And Bob wasn't about to look stupid—especially in front of the boss! He had worked at this company too long and too hard to hamper his reputation. And in another five years, after being at PanAm for a decade, he would be locked in for his retirement.

Bob had approached the women a few times. He really appreciated their attitude in the meetings. Especially after Tom's latest stunt, he expected an all-out war from the ladies. But they had remained remarkably professional. It's like they had some force field protecting them. They didn't react to Tom or the other negativity like most people did.

HR had reined Tom in a bit, but he was still cocky as all hell. But isn't that sales? Isn't that the way it goes? He really didn't need to lose two of his best directors at the same time due to Tom's behavior. And he knew they were both top talent.

Bob reflected over the last few months. He had seen Laura and Gertrude being very strategic. They came into the leadership meetings often together and then split up, sitting across from each other at the Board room table. There was a complete change in their responses. No more undercutting or criticizing. If this kind of behavior started in the meeting, it appeared that they simply didn't participate. There had been some kind of nonverbal communication going on during those times of ugliness for years but they stopped engaging in it.

It wasn't like they had withdrawn or even gone passive-aggressive. They often offered alternative solutions that put the group back on track. But if the ugliness started getting out of control, they simply waited it out, remaining calm. Somehow, they had drastically reduced their reactivity. You could see it on their faces. You could even see it in how they walked down the hall.

Bob decided he wanted some of that! It was time to really start finding out what was going on. He would start with them separately. Maybe one of the ladies would spill.

Gertrude was at her desk preparing for her presentation at the next day's leadership meeting. She was actually excited and energized. She knew the ideas she and her team were developing were good, innovative, and a bit edgy. When she was out of the shit, she loved developing new ideas and the graphics and copy to support them.

As she looked up, she saw a familiar face standing quietly at her door, waiting for her attention. It was Bob. He looked a bit drawn and quiet. Her smile invited him in, and he shut the door behind him. Gertrude could sense something was wrong but stayed light in her tone. "So, what's up?" she asked him.

Bob began with a tale of fear Gertrude knew was still apart of PanAm. As he spoke, his life energy appeared to drain out of him. Gertrude knew better than to comment. She knew he would say he was fine.

Bob had come to work here a few years after Gertrude and Laura. He was one of the better ones; he at least had moments of kindness. He tried to help make work fun and appeared to really care about his people. But he was totally caught in the toxic system—like a fish unable to see the water.

Laura, Gertrude, and Bob had all been to lunch a few times over the last five years. They had had some interesting and intense discussions about the nature of leadership and even a bit about the new science. But it was all talk. Even when the company sent them to leadership seminars, nothing ever changed.

Bob began, "Hey Gertrude, I know there is something different with you and Laura. I have seen the changes over the last few months. What's going on?"

Gertrude smiled. The moment had appeared. It was time to let Bob know what they were up to. She said, "We were wondering when you were going to ask. Actually, it's pretty big. We decided to take all that leadership training you have sent us to and actually use it. We have taken it deeper. But mostly, we have done as you asked us to do."

Bob's eyes widened in surprise. "I am not sure what training you are talking about."

"Yeah, well, it's probably the integration into our daily work that has it all really coming together. But we are following the science and leadership literature. You know how Laura and I love to read; and we go to leadership training every year. Well, it turns out, we rock at integration, too!"

Bob's reaction of quiet shock remained.

"Bob, this is big, Laura said. "We have done something few people are able to do. We are happy to share, but we are not willing to be a target for any more of Tom's BS. So, if you really want to know and are willing to truly listen and learn, then we should get a time on the calendar, maybe a lunch away from this place. This is going to take a while."

Bob sighed. He was a bit taken aback by such a strong response from Gertrude. Being a complex guy, Bob was hoping it was something really simple. But he knew she wasn't wrong. "Okay. I am ready to listen," Bob said.

Gertrude opened their shared calendar. "Let's see, how about lunch on Friday with Laura?" Bob agreed and headed back down the hall. Gertrude sent the calendar invite to the three of them.

Gertrude was struck by the level of pain Bob appeared to be in, he looked so pale and exhausted. She began to feel selfish for not letting him in sooner. *Oops,* she thought, *none of that. Guilt takes me out of coherence.* She shifted her attention to her breath and refocused. Friday was just a few days away.

Chapter 9

Calvin was the company's chief engineer. He had started in broadcasting as a production assistant in a small midwestern market. He had stayed in the field his entire career and had seen some outlandish stuff. He had actually walked into the studio one evening to see two newscasters dry humping each other on the news desk. After that, he knew he had seen it all.

After finishing college, Calvin wasn't going back to Mississippi. There was no opportunity there. As an African-American, he had fought his way up the so-called ladder and dealt with discrimination, aggression, and full-on racism along the way. He had learned to play the game of politics that was embedded in every system he had worked in. As chief engineer, he had to attend all ridiculous leadership meetings and knew that they were the norm.

But something was up. Something was different. And it somehow involved Laura and Gertrude. Things were changing, actually getting better. There had been some big shit-shows lately, but the Laura and Gertrude had handled all of them, remaining calmer than he ever would have.

He liked Gertrude and Laura. They did their jobs, listened, and discussed problems. He knew that if they were involved in an issue, it would get resolved with a minimum of grandstanding. He asked Bob about this

A Call to Wholeness

change-for-the-better in the meetings, but it was clear that Bob didn't really get it. Now, there was a two-hour lunch with Bob, Gertrude, and Laura showing up on the corporate calendar, so, just maybe, Bob was going to find out. If so, Calvin definitely wanted to be included.

"Hey Laura," Calvin said, as he leaned against her door frame.

"Hey Calvin. We have your expense report. You should have your check by Friday," Laura replied.

"Thanks, Laura. I know you've got that covered. But that's not why I'm here. Can I ask you, what's this Friday's meeting all about?"

"Oh, Friday," Laura said with a smile. "We are thinking of going paddleboarding after work." She teasingly batted her eyelashes at Calvin, attempting to look innocent.

Calvin laughed out loud. "Sure! I'm not buying that! So, come clean with me: What's really going on?"

Laura waved Calvin into her office, smiled again, and looked him straight in the eye. She knew he was one of the good ones. He'd had their backs so many times. She decided to offer up a bit of information. "Okay, here is the simplest explanation. Gertrude and I decided to step out of the toxicity and create a better work life for ourselves—to actually operate from our stated values and offer real leadership. It started out of desperation and has grown into so much more than we could have ever imagined. I'm sure you can guess why we have not shared. We don't need a bigger target on our backs."

Calvin nodded. "I knew something was up, but I couldn't figure it out. I did suspect that you two were behind it. Can you tell me more?"

"Well, we are the only ones. It's actually been pretty fun," Laura added.

"You know you can trust me," Calvin was quick to add. "Is there is some way I can help? After all, anything that makes this place saner is just the ticket. I would jump on that bandwagon. How can I help?"

Just then Gertrude knocked on the door and peeked in. When she saw the look on Laura's face, she stepped in the room and shut the door behind her. Calvin looked back and forth between the women, and, in turn, they looked at Calvin wordlessly.

"My, my. You sure are sly! What's more, you both sure know how to keep a secret! Even more, I like what you've done," Calvin offered very cheekily, concluding, "I really hope you'll deal me in. Do let me know how I can help." He then left Laura's office.

The seriousness of the moment hit Laura. She said, "Okay, it's obviously time to share and figure out how to move this further into the organization. Calvin would be a great advocate to have!"

"I hadn't even been thinking about adding Calvin," Gertrude responded. "I knew we would eventually have to let Bob in—he is our boss after all. I like Calvin. I trust Calvin, but as we were talking with him about our intention, I began to get a bit panicky, moving this into the organization . . . that's kind of scary."

Laura added, "Calvin is a good fit for our expansion and I definitely trust him. At the same time, all the turf war issues are being triggered up in me, too. I know we are part of Wholeness and we have done a great job understanding all of this. But now, my fear response seems more real than Wholeness. The only way I can think to explain it to Calvin and Bob is in combative language. How do we work from Wholeness and explain these ideas to people who have a completely different worldview?"

"Okay, we know this is a normal part of resetting our reflexes. There will be times that the events and our reactions seem more real. But this is how we strengthen our knowing of Wholeness. So, let's just walk it through," Gertrude suggested.

She continued, "I really liked our little happy bubble. How do we go forward without it bursting? I am happy about this development, but it scares me, too. I know part of this is my internal reflex, but the level of shit could go up one hundred times if we are not careful."

Laura offered, "Looks like the first thing to do is to bring ourselves all the way back to peace and then look at the situation from there. We need to be intentional about how we set our own field."

"Yes, of course. Dinner on my patio?" Gertrude asked.

"Sure, it's been working for us so far," Laura said. "But let's walk DB in the forest first. It speeds up our ability to come back into balance."

Gertrude smiled. She was definitely ready to be filled with color and light again.

Chapter 10

The ladies were walking down the path, a deeper sense of connection beginning to be restored.

"I think the guys would respond better if we put a name to our system. I have an idea that just popped into my head: holographic leadership. It will make it easier to explain things and puts even more emphasis on Wholeness," said Laura.

"I like it!" Gertrude exclaimed. "It reminds us of our Interconnection. *Holographic* means we can view multiple perspectives at once, it allows us to resolve paradox more easily, and to clearly see the patterns and synchronicities within the Whole. That's really important."

"Yeah, it really puts the emphasis on being able to expand our perception and think more clearly," Laura replied.

At the end of the walk, the ladies knew they needed to include Calvin. He was a great fit. In the lady's experience, Calvin was more aware than all the other leaders.

Friday morning, the ladies prepared with a longer sit in silence and deeper commitment to Wholeness, trusting Bob and Calvin, and surrendering to the outcome. Anticipating their presentation to the men over lunch, it felt more important than anything they had ever done in the leadership meeting. They really wanted it to go well.

But before lunch was the 10:00 AM weekly leadership meeting and Tom was in full form. He was blaming everyone else for his team's mistakes. The ladies stayed calm and observed. They remembered to see Tom as a legitimate participant in this meeting. They remembered he was a good negotiator and successful at his job. It was all beginning to make more sense. Tom was a legitimate participant; it was his behavior they had been reacting to.

Laura and Gertrude could also both see a light in Bob's and Calvin's eyes. Bob watched how strong the women were, how steady they were holding. It was a sight to see. This had been happening right in front of him for months, and he was just really seeing it for the first time. The moment for this luncheon was perfect!

Calvin was beginning to feel cautiously optimistic. He had been working so long in this environment, he had become numb. Now, there was more awareness around the issues. Everyone he knew worked in some kind of crazy environment. *It was the norm, right?* Now, he was beginning to have a glimmer of hope, a possible alternative, one based in respect.

The ladies left the building first and were able to snag a back corner table at their favorite Italian restaurant. The bit of privacy was good; no one was eavesdropping or putting on a show.

After they all ordered, Laura began to explain what they were doing. "Okay, so I'm sure you both remember from all those leadership trainings that our number one task as a leader is to hold the environment—the culture for the productivity we wish to see. We have taken that much deeper than the leadership literature suggests.

The process begins with our own state: heart, mind, and body. If the leader is in a coherent state, she offers coherence to her employees. If she is out of coherence, she significantly contributes to each employee's chaos. A coherent internal state allows the group to synchronize, to align together.

"The primary contribution made by each and every person is her presence, the frequency from which she operates. Think of an EKG machine. There is a strong physiological piece to change, which makes sustainable organizational change an internal process. The habits of an organization are held within each person. It is the commitment of each person to his and her development that allows an organization to jump out of the current reality of how business is run."

"So, basically, we have learned that this process is one of integration—coherence in one's physiology brings balance to one's feelings, opening ways to override powerful habits, 'rewire' our brains, and integrate our mental capacities with our hearts. We now know how to alter the biochemical responses of our emotional reflexes and integrate our abstract mental capacities with our heart, allowing us to stay aligned with our values and act from integrity, even in the middle of a shitshow."

Gertrude and Laura laughed at the look on Bob's face, shocked and surprised.

"Okay," Laura said, smiling, "I'm screwing with you a bit. We felt like we needed to come in, science blazing. We know you are more likely to listen to two women if we sound pedantic. Oh, another really important aspect of this work is deep reality testing. That means we call out the sexism and the prejudice. We don't pretend it's not there. We can't change patterns we can't see or are not willing to look at. That is actually one of the toughest parts, to really see what is going on and face it."

"Wow! That's really deep," Calvin responded. "I can support that. While I can track most of what you're saying, what really matters to me are the results. That is what I want. I can see a positive difference already—especially in our hostile system that stresses you AND me! This blows my mind; and I see that I can learn from what you're doing. I see that people can make a difference—even in an environment that is toxic to folks like me. I can learn from y'all."

"Yes," Gertrude added. We have actively been integrating all the reading and seminars from the last ten years. So, there is a lot you already know. The best part is when we expanded things to include the new science, we found a way to step out of the toxicity. We have learned to keep ourselves in balance and it feels so much better. Another challenge is retraining ourselves in how we see. The more present and coherent we are, the more we can work from interconnection.

"Wholeness is. Our universe is interconnected at a very deep level. This makes so much more sense when we remember everything is energy. Science has known this for over a hundred years. Yet, we continue to condition our thoughts to break-up our perception of Wholeness. We have literally been taught to cut things into pieces and see them as separate. But we are not separate. The more incoherent our physiology, the more fragmented our thoughts and the more distorted our perception, the more reactive our behavior becomes," Gertrude summarized.

Laura added, "That's actually a pretty good summary of this whole organization: incoherent, fragmented, distorted and reactive. It's probably ninety-five percent of the others too; and we actually call that normal." She shook her head, then continued, "Wow, how sick is that? Now that I am out of that pattern, there is no way I am going back! I still get caught in it sometimes, but I no longer believe it needs to be our reality.

"The old system of thinking and acting is woven into us, as is racism and sexism and all 'isms.' This way of being is allowing perception to unravel, piercing our awareness so we can choose differently. It is not a speed race; it is a sustainable, consistent, chosen path. Strong conscious action is better than frantic reaction. This is what we need to be in order to help each other out of the crazy shit we call normal."

Gertrude interjected, "So what we are talking about is a complete shift in how we look at an organization. How we hold ourselves accountable. How we define change and what it means to actually operate from a values-based leadership perspective, not just talk about it."

Laura asked, "What's your response to that? Do you still want to know the rest, or do you need plausible deniability?" Both women smiled and waited for a response.

Calvin was deep in thought, taking it all in, his head turning with each new interaction, as if he was watching a tennis match at Wimbledon.

"Wow!" Bob said, "that's a lot. I can see how you needed time and needed to be careful. I do respect both of you. Actually, the three of you are the core of my leadership team. You show up. You are professional. And you help to reduce the shitshow. So please hear this from me. Great job! You make my work easier."

He added, "I really saw your impact in today's meeting. For the first time, I realized you are doing it all on purpose. It was impressive. I may not understand it all yet, but it's working. You have significantly improved the quality of our work and the key performance indicators. I can't argue with that. You said you took it step by step, learning as you went. I think that sounds like a good approach."

"I like that step-by-step approach, too," Calvin said. ":This is the simplest explanation for organizational change I can remember.

Mostly, I have seen some big production with a bunch of rules and changes in behavior, but no real change in the way we think or the system itself."

"It would help to have an overall outline of the course; I work better with a grasp of the big picture. But let's dig in and start like you ladies did, step by step," Bob added.

"That sounds good," Calvin agreed.

"Okay, let me give you the briefest of outlines," Gertrude suggested. "We have decided to call it holographic leadership as Wholeness is critical to understanding and working from it. Holographic leadership integrates value-based leadership into an understanding of an energetic, holographic world—a world where the unseen is the primary influencer. Wholeness is the deep interconnection and the basis of our understanding in physics today, including holographic theory."

"The process," she continued, "begins with intention. We have one we created; we can email it to you. Then there is the internal self-management piece. I have found an easier way than the way we started. It's called HeartMath; and it helps with all the chaos, here and now. HeartMath created a set of techniques that teach us how to reset our autonomic nervous system. This is critical for getting out of our mind chatter and unhealthy reactions. The best part is that you can do it while you walk down the hall. It's a totally on-demand system and only takes about five sessions to learn."

Gertrude picked up, "Being able to see our reactions as an old habit is also big. When we are in reactionary mode, we are absolutely sure what we are perceiving is real. We can't see alternative possibilities until we get out of our fight, flight, or freeze state. So, having a way to break our patterns is huge. The courage and willingness to see our patterns and shift them is the hard work. Building physical coherence is critical. Holographic leadership is built on our physiology as leaders."

"Breaking my old habits works perfectly with my silence practice. The meditation practice is important because it takes me to Wholeness, helping me know the vastness that is beyond my spinning mind. Silence helps me realize there is an 'I' that is separate from my running thoughts, that my reactions are not all of me. Then, only after we learn to manage and take care of ourselves individually can we, as a group, begin using this practice we call Dialogue. Dialogue allows for people with diverse perspectives to discuss topics that are important to them where all parties feel safe and respected no matter how great their differences or points of view. It is possible for people who strongly disagree with one another's views to still have an opportunity to learn from one another without feeling forced to either protect or change their opinions. Laura and I are learning this part now. It is definitely a big component; otherwise we get stuck in our own head and old behaviors."

"Wow, you two have really thought about this!" Calvin exclaimed. "I didn't really think this was possible. I definitely had no hope of fixing anything. But now, I can see how it all fits together. Laura and I went to that leadership training last year on value-based leadership; and I can see now how those values apply here. I know they talked about holding steady, but there was nothing specific to help us actually do it. I can see now how using meditation and mindfulness techniques combined with biophysical training make it possible. I like the idea of Wholeness. It helps me remember that it's not all about me! I also see the huge change in how you two lead. You invite input while making sure that folks don't get out of hand. I've done that myself, but not as consciously as you. I really like this new way: holographic leadership. I want to learn more! When do we start our master classes?" He smiled.

"It sounds like we start with intention and learning to be more self-aware and coherent," Bob said. "And we take better care of ourselves? My doctor would like that."

"Yes, you got it!" Laura said and laughed. "At least you have us helping and modeling. You don't have to figure it all out for yourself, you know, like we did."

Gertrude added, "Laura and I can come up with an outline of all the steps and will add our intention. The intention is really the overall frame and will help you see the big picture. How does that sound, Laura?"

"Sure, we can do that," replied Laura. "It will be a great exercise in critical thinking to see how the pieces have come together. It took a bit longer at the beginning for us; we had to decide how to do this and then continually show up, despite all the toxicity in the organization triggering us."

"Yeah," Gertrude agreed. "The instinct to protect ourselves is still strong. Even as we share this with you right now, there is still a niggle of concern. But we are saving massive time and energy. And are so much happier! Look at our teams and how well they are working together. Look at the ease in communications and problem solving in our departments!"

"No doubt! I've seen those changes with my own eyes," Calvin weighed in. "Looks like we're goin' to town!"

As Bob drove back to the station, he was hopeful for the first time in a long time. He was also shocked. He wasn't expecting this level of thought and research behind what the ladies were doing. *Is my reaction misogyny? I had better start paying more attention,* he thought.

Bob continued reflecting on the meeting. He had listened to all the women had said and it seemed doable. *Could this work for a larger group with people not as close as Gertrude and Laura?* he wondered. He knew which people on the leadership team would try to sabotage change. *There is some real risk assessment that needed to be done here. How could this be taken into the organization? Would the four of us be enough? The ladies have already effected change and done some risk management. I always thought change had to be bulldozed through, 'Create a sense of urgency,' how many times have I heard that? I don't want any more urgency. I don't need any more stress. What Laura and Gertrude are doing is so different. And yet, it is working. It has actually reduced the drama.*

I like Calvin's participation. He's solid and steady with more experience than any of us. His input and support will be invaluable. For now, it will be the four of them. This feels comfortable. Boy, these ladies brought it to the table. I really have some work to do. And I actually feel excited to do it . . . imagine that.

Gertrude and Laura left work after the lunch meeting. The journey of taking their big ideas into the organization had begun. Time to celebrate! It was a beautiful day, so they decided to get a jump start on the art fair to kick off the weekend.

Both were full of enthusiasm and in awe of what was happening. It was so much simpler than either ever expected. It also was scary, putting themselves out there. It could go south very quickly. But so far, so good.

Chapter 11

As Laura and Gertrude sat down to write the outline, they pulled back to look at all they had experienced in the last six months. Both instinctively knew that modeling this new way of being was the most important path right now, holding clear and calm, allowing and listening deep within, feeling and knowing the insights and intuition, and taking care of themselves, staying in balance.

The process offered them the reflective space necessary for critical thinking and clear reality testing. Their spinning minds had slowed down, their awareness heightened. These shifts had increased their willingness to connect with the team and listen more deeply. Even as the situation around them remained relatively the same.

Moving away from the constant state of defending and fighting translated into increasing capacity by taking responsibility even at the most difficult times. It gave them the ability to focus on what is important and not get lost in biochemical reflexes and emotional reactions.

The following Monday morning, the ladies emailed the outline. There was also an email from Tom to the entire team, slandering Calvin and his department for "mistakes" in airing "his commercials." Toxicity in all its glory on full display!

"Wow, the timing is unbelievable. Tom's email clearly demonstrates exactly the level of self-centeredness that is going on around here," Gertrude said to Laura.

"Perception is a powerful thing. You can actually tell Tom really believes this is what happened," Laura said as she shook her head in dismay.

Calvin showed up at Laura's office, rage in his eyes. "Okay ladies, this email is full on bullshit. I am ready to get started. Help me work this new plan, before I go beat the shit out of him."

"Let's call Bob and create a plan together," Laura said, then picked up the phone. "Rule one, everybody can't lose it at the same time. Check, we have that one. Calvin, know we have your back. Bob can do this at ten. For now, let's get you breathing. Focus on the area of your chest and imagine yourself breathing in appreciation."

Calvin looked at her like she was nuts.

Laura laughed. "Okay, that's a bridge too far. Let's just start with the breathing. Nice and steady breaths; they don't need to be too deep. You can focus on how much you appreciate our support."

Gertrude smiled, then said, "This is an opportunity to directly take on the toxicity without creating more. We get to do what we agreed to last Friday. This is how it's done; we have to interrupt the pattern and act differently. Yes, we are ready to support you and most importantly not shame Tom."

In the end, they all discussed the issue, used the new model and were able to gain a greater sense of calm. All agreed that the email didn't pose an immediate crisis and would be addressed by Calvin and Bob before the meeting on Friday. This gave some time for Calvin to get centered. They also agreed the men would join the ladies at their Friday breakfast meetings. Dealing with this latest round of toxicity would be their first case study. Turns out the men were just as affected by the BS as the ladies.

The breakfast meeting allowed the four to use the model with a real-life situation. Gertrude jumped into the explanation: "It's like this. Every thought I think is not the truth. We can see this in Tom's email, but often not in ourselves. If my mind is constantly running, I can't see how I have fixated on a particular point of view. I just keep thinking the same thoughts and believe they are true. Calvin even your reaction was a habitual response. Your anger is valid; but here, in this meeting, we are looking at our habits of reacting and thinking. That is why we have a clear intention—to align our actions, especially when we're angry. Laura and I have learned to step out of our anger—our spinning minds through letting go. Well, most of the time," Gertrude added with a smile.

Gertrude continued. "So basically, we have a clear intention. We are aware of and manage our state as often as possible and then suspend our reaction and thoughts to see alternatives that line up better with our intention. The recentering technique helps with this. There is also a technique called tapping, or the emotional freedom technique, aka EFT. HeartMath and EFT help break up locked-in patterns. Without being able to change the physical state that locks in our responses, we don't really have a chance to create a change within the organization. This is the opportunity we have right now to reduce the toxicity within PanAm. We are working from an intention of Wholeness, which means real interconnection and inclusion. Literally everything is energetically interwoven. We look for ways to support people, even the ones we don't like or 'who don't deserve it.' If we separate someone out, we are in judgment, out of coherence, and not working from Wholeness. It comes down to who we choose to be and how we choose to treat others.

"Together, we've got this! We are interrupting our reactions. We are in a process of becoming and developing. Our behavior and reactions are about us; we can't be triggered by Tom if we didn't have a wound already there. We do this for ourselves. In reality, this works. If we can't suspend our thoughts, we can't break our patterns. We can't lead when we are triggered in a fight/flight/freeze response. The leadership seminars didn't teach us this."

The men were looking saturated, so Laura suggested they read through the outline. "We have a clear plan to follow up with Tom, and you two have a place to start. It may become a bit overwhelming in the midst of all our regular work. But just relax and choose again, realign to our commitment to be the kind of organization we say we are, in synch with our values and vision statement. Day by day, we show up and build a new culture. This process offers the steps and helps build our capacity to actually align with who we say we are. But it's up to each of us individually to actually resynch, moment to moment."

Gertrude jumped in. "This is not about perfection. It's about self-authoring, owning who we are and what shows up in our lives. We manage our state of mind and behavior and correct as soon as we can. Our intention helps us increase our awareness. This is a consciousness practice. We bring ourselves back to the present and self-correct. We both use the HeartMath system. It's very practical for a work setting, and we can do it as we walk down the hall. There is a directory of providers to teach you.

"You can also see this is the essence of emotional intelligence. We act from self-awareness and interconnection. We develop our capacities for interpersonal relationships. We need to work from trust and give the trust time to deepen. The old way of pushing through doesn't work. Laura's term for this is *harden off*. We let it grow strong within the four of us, and then there will be a moment, just like with you two, for us to take it bigger."

Sitting in the next leadership meeting, Calvin wasn't clear and calm. He was still pissed about the latest attack on his team. He took a deep breath and let go some more of his resistance. *Holographic leadership. Interconnection. Seeing Tom as part of the Whole* . . . This was Calvin's new mantra. It was taking all his professionalism. But he respected Laura and Gertrude too much to blow it off. And maybe for the first time, he was not alone. He felt included with this new system he was learning. He knew he had a safe place to influence, discuss, share, and even vent. It wasn't *this* meeting, but it existed. His voice was heard. It felt good. If these ideas had come from the CEO, he would have assumed "flavor of the month." But from the ladies and this internal grassroots process it felt very real.

Calvin had watched the ladies teach Bob about sexism and misogyny. He enjoyed that. He had put up with plenty—including racism, but he had seen many guys treat a woman like their personal sex toy. He had some sharing to do also. But in an atmosphere of respect, it wasn't so bad. There was some traction happening. It wasn't all for show. And he didn't have to go first, Calvin was relieved. He could see the ladies' level of commitment. He would stand with them. We were doing this!

The weekend flew by, and everyone was back at it again. Gertrude hadn't been part of Bob's discussions with Tom, and to his credit he wasn't sharing. She could see the effect of increased accountability. The drama was dialed down a bit, and her department was feeling less tense. Work felt 'normal' or what she thought normal should feel like. People were more pleasant and focused. There was a bit of space to share a story or have a laugh.

This week, the originally scheduled Friday morning training session with Bob, Calvin, Gertrude, and Laura was moved up to Thursday, and they all agreed to go to lunch. It was another beautiful fall day, the four of them decided to sit outside to enjoy the color and crisp breeze. There was a newfound appreciation of simple things, as they each developed their capacity to be more present.

"Let's all take a few breaths and bring ourselves and our attention to this moment," Gertrude began.

"We can do a quick review of the outline we sent you," Laura said. "After we figured out that Wholeness is real and we can align with it at work, we created an intention, a focal point of our highest hope that is here in the outline. It is actually a bit more than being emotionally intelligent. But that is what it looks like on the surface. We aren't going to remember this every moment. We work from where we are. So, when we are out of coherence, we bring ourselves back into balance. This includes helping each other recognize when we are reacting and move back into center. This is literally holding steady, internally and externally. If I am responsible for my state, I am less passive-aggressive and all the other crap we see here at PanAm.

"This works because it is not behavior modification. We are not placing our attention out there and fixing others, or even using our will to force change in our own behavior. It's simply a shift in our attention, continually asking ourselves, what is my state? How do I return to balance? We keep our focus internal. So, let's do a quick review of the outline.

"Our intention is to work from Wholeness and interconnection; sensing and knowing there is a solution embedded within every problem. Be responsible for our own internal state and the impact we have on the organization. Commit to our own development and bring ourselves back into coherence, moment to moment. Support each other through this process. Silence and mindfulness builds our internal capacity as we move out into the organization. Step out of our limited self into an expanding sense of Wholeness.

The first steps for you newbies are to begin to gain awareness of your mental and emotional patterns and to be clear on the intention of interconnection. What does that mean for you? Laura and I have different views, but we have no problem accepting each other. We both know Wholeness by any other name is just as loving. So, pick what works for you; this is an internal process. The gifts it brings show up in our work. From here we show up and practice every day."

Gertrude continued, "One of the things Laura and I did at the beginning while we were deepening our practice was to review our favorite parts of the leadership literature. We were reminded of a couple of big points. First, that Wholeness has already been introduced into leadership; and growing up is necessary. Leadership is not yelling and spewing our emotional state on our people. It's aligning, motivating, and influencing them toward a common good. Up to now, our culture has been following whoever screams the loudest. Value-based leadership is different. It's not based on a greed model of business, pushing, and shoving at all costs. It's not about making money any way we can; the means do not justify the end. That by itself is a big deal!

"Value-based leadership is about the common good. Unfortunately, going to a day of training, even if we do it every year, doesn't help us really initiate change, especially with our current workloads. As leaders of this organization, it's up to us to hold an environment for the change we want to see. And to do that we have to hold steady and continually get ourselves into balance, in coherence. We have to take care of ourselves. We can't make novel, innovative decisions when we are stressed out. If we are crazy, our people will be crazy."

"Isn't that the truth," Calvin agreed.

Gertrude went further, "This old greed model is deeply embedded in our culture, our thinking, and our behavior. We are already working on being more aware about shifting our habits. Our habits of behavior are what will create our environment—the standards of what is acceptable here at PanAm. We are responsible for setting those standards for everyone. We do that by how we act. The way we behave becomes part of our culture. Laura and I have been holding clear and calm for a few months now, and it's having an impact in our departments.

"We are listening better. Like Dialogue, value-based leadership definitely includes listening to all the voices. A culture of respect allows and actually encourages quieter voices to speak. In fact, it's required that, as leaders of this organization, we create a safe environment for all voices to be heard.

"We are also responsible for making sure we are directing attention—theirs and ours—to the priorities. That's Wholeness and the realities of the day, realigning moment to moment with our intention to our vision. Checking our attention can easily be added to those moments we all take to recenter. So, we aren't stacking more to do; it's paired with something we are already doing."

"Oh yeah; that's good. I can see that," Bob said. "When I take ninety seconds to bring myself back, I also do a quick internal check-in in my head about what's happening in the organization and make any quick adjustments. That is certainly easier than cleaning up a big blow out, especially, if it's one of mine." Bob laughed at himself. "I don't always remember this. But I can see how, with repetition and support, it will come."

"Yeah, that's right, Bob," Laura agreed. "We keep showing up, allowing the new pattern and the new culture to build. We can create a moment to align in our meetings, like we just did. Taking time to model that internal check-in as a way to recenter ourselves. From there, we can also make sure we are communicating and giving everyone the information they need to do their job. As issues come up, we check ourselves to see how we can do better. We correct ourselves first, then our employee, if it's even necessary.

"It's up to us to frame the issue in the way our employees can understand and has meaning toward our goals. So yes, all those critical key performance indicators Tom is always talking about are important. We are changing how we lead, and we need to meet our goals. This is why I can begin to see Tom as valuable. He is the one paying attention to our sales numbers and of course we need that."

Calvin interjected. "I can see that. It's not always easy to remember when he's being an ass."

"Yes," Laura replied, "and it's our job to align with what we want to see, not get in his face. We all have done that at some point and this self-correction is a big one for all of us. There will be conflict. Remember, respectful, orchestrated conflict is healthy. It makes our organization stronger. There is no better way to listen to all of the voices than to create a space where even opposing views can be shared. It's actually good for the organization."

Gertrude jumped in. "Another opportunity we have here is to extend the responsibility of making decisions. We need to share leadership duties to allow more development and greater buy-in. We can offer opportunities for everyone learn and grow. So, yes, that's delegation. And we build capacity, allowing others to offer ideas and to 'fail' gracefully.

"You can see there is a natural fit here between value based leadership and everyone's development. Our practice helps us grow up. It also helps us be calmer and think better. It's actually a big deal. Think about it. When we are shut down, there's no agility or creativity. We get less work done. The same is true for our employees. No one develops well in toxicity. It's all CYA.

"It's such a simple explanation, Gertrude! I remember learning about most of this at our last annual training seminar. And I can see how these tasks all fit with what we are doing," Bob added. "I can see why mindfulness and silence are so important. If we can't manage ourselves, how can we manage others?"

"Well said, Bob," Laura added. "Calvin, let's sit down and talk about how we can take this into the meeting with Tom. This last incident needs to be cleaned up and clear boundaries set. Can you do 4:00 PM today?"

Calvin replied, "That works for me. Then hopefully, we can talk with Tom tomorrow. I will work on shifting my state and keeping my responses in check. The meeting will be a good first step in working from respect and holding myself in balance."

"That's great, Calvin. And I will work on listening better. I guess we are learning together," Bob said.

The next day, Bob and Calvin met with Tom. Bob was happy with how prepared, calm, and clear he felt. He got the expected pushback initially still was able to set clear guidelines. Tom seemed surprised by the direct conversation but was cooperative in the meeting. He actually was much less resistant than either Bob or Calvin had expected. The conversation was productive with everyone appreciating the clarity that emerged.

Chapter 12

For two months now, Bob and Calvin have been practicing the individual techniques, increasing their capacity to hold steady. The Friday morning training sessions with the foursome continued to develop their self-awareness, self-authoring, and value-based leadership. It was the one place they could all truly relax, be themselves, and discuss ideas and challenges.

Their presence was being felt around the organization. Communication was clearer and accountability was increasing with respectful directness. The space for disagreement and collaboration was expanding. The BS was diminishing as old behaviors were addressed. Tom seemed to have put his head down and was lying low.

The ladies were once again in the forest walking DB. It had been a great week. "What a good life!" Gertrude said. She was feeling peace and in her happy place. DB was prancing just ahead of them, occasionally pausing, ears perked. Every ten minutes or so, DB would stop and sit almost as if prompting Gertrude and Laura to listen to the call of Wholeness.

"Yes," Laura said, "it feels like we are rebuilding the culture layer by layer, taking our time, allowing it to emerge. I love that we are able to discover the next step without it being imposed on us by the powers that be. Our attention is strong and goal focused. We are agile enough to be able to adjust as needed in the moment. This is a lot easier since, you know, we are actually present in the moment." She laughed.

"Yeah," Gertrude offered, "it is allowing and responding to what is needed, not what we think needs to happen, or 'should' happen. I think this openness, this willingness to not know everything from the beginning, is a very significant part of the process. It's like we are leaning into Wholeness and She is leaning into us."

Laura smiled, "I like that, leaning into Wholeness."

The workweek started peacefully. Projects were flowing and goals being met. Calvin was getting the hang of this internal state management thing. He had not realized it was making such a difference until his kids commented that he was listening better. Any time a teenager says something like that, it's a big win. He had discussed the process with his wife. She loved it and appreciated the energy he still had when he got home. She even wanted constant updates so she could take it into her work.

Calvin's department was running smoother. Of course, it was a great help that Tom was finally being held accountable. No one got in Tom's face, most importantly not Calvin. His engineers really seemed to appreciate the accountability and the clearer communication.

"Hey everyone," Calvin greeted his team as he joined the Friday morning training session. "I am ready for my moment of calm. And as a quick check-in, I can tell you this process has already begun impacting my family. My wife wants updates so she can take some of these ideas into her workplace; and my teenage son even said I was listening better!"

"Wow, that's great Calvin! That is the kind of thing that keeps us going when we can't remember why we are doing it." Bob chuckled and everyone laughed.

"It would be great if your wife did this with you, Calvin. It only makes it easier to hold. I know having Gertrude at the beginning of this process was critical for me," Laura emphasized.

Everyone stopped for a minute to collect their energy and attention, and of course, reset their autonomic nervous system.

"Okay, as we keep building our capacity," Gertrude started, "a silence practice is the next big piece. It helps us break our addiction and attachment to our spinning thoughts. When we can step back, we can begin to feel Wholeness in a way that feels so much more real. Interconnection is more actual. It means we can find our center, grounded in the here and now. It reminds us it's not 'all about me.' It also allows us to begin to know wisdom and to listen to our intuition. Moving into deep wisdom is state dependent. We can only know Wholeness from silence. We can only really lead from clarity. Otherwise, we are back muddled in our current mood, confusing it with reality.

"It doesn't matter which practice you choose. Pick one that resonates with you, aligned with your beliefs. What matters is we sit in silence regardless of whether it's a 'good' or 'bad' day. We are learning to allow—to surrender—while being clear on our intention. Silence helps our clarity. We learn to shift our state to use both our vision and logic to create our world.

"Perfection is an illusion of command-and-control leadership. It has never been real; it's an impossible standard. The same is true for a perfectly quiet mind. That is not our goal. What matters is to regularly surrender our mind chatter. Allow Wholeness space. Until we can step out of our limited self, we can't see how we impact our people, our company or our world."

"You are both doing well, bringing yourselves into coherence, interrupting your reactions. Now, you can begin to explore and find your silence practice," Gertrude smiled. "And we are here, ready to support you both."

Calvin thanked Gertrude. "That totally lines up with what I experienced this last weekend. So, I just sit in silence for how long?"

Winking, Laura shared something she learned from the meditation class she and Gertrude took together and shared it with Calvin. "According to Buddha, one should sit and meditate for twenty minutes each day. Unless you are too busy; then you should sit for two hours."

Laura continued, "But really, we can only start with where we are, Calvin. So where are you? Is it five minutes, and you add from there? Or ten minutes or even two minutes? It is all good. Start where you are. We are allowing this to build, not forcing something through. For me, it is easiest if I commit to a recurring time each day. Not a time on the clock, but a place in my routine. When I first get up works best for me and that differs like when I'm on vacation."

"Wow, on vacation too? I guess it makes sense; it would only help me relax faster," Calvin mused aloud.

"Yes, this goes beyond work for me; it's who I choose to be," Laura said. "So, yes; it's critical to improving how we work—and it really impacts all of me. How could it not? To think that what we do in one area of our life would not affect another seems to me to be a fragmented way of thinking, right? It's what you already said, Calvin; it impacts all parts of life."

The next leadership team meeting synced up in a way that felt as smooth as silk. There was clarity, respect, and productivity. Tom seemed a bit stunned. He would try to trigger people with almost no response. With Bob, Calvin, Gertrude, and Laura holding clear and calm, all the others followed. Tom was no longer in control of the room or the culture.

Chapter 13

Bob felt like he was actually leading, maybe for the first time ever in his career. In addition to the intention of Wholeness, he was using the company vision and values to align his decision-making and discussions with his employees. He had even begun using them in discussions with the CEO. Everything felt more congruent and his staff seemed to appreciate his clear communication. He had even had a few direct conversations with Tom and his antics were quieting down. There was conflict, but Bob more consciously orchestrated the conversation instead of ignoring it or shutting it down. It turned out that having respectful conversations actually helped more creative ideas to emerge.

Thanksgiving had them skipping a week of their group training sessions. Bob really missed the opportunity to connect with his three colleagues. The practices, discussions, and support of the others really energized him. Collaboration, the new ideas, and figuring out how it all applied to PanAm was actually a lot of fun. The excitement was palpable. It took thirty minutes for them to share what had happened over the last two weeks.

Calvin couldn't remember anything like it. He was happy about being part of such a great group. He continued to feel respected and included. It was an honor to have these two ladies quietly leading them into a different culture.

"Hey, guys," Gertrude said, "I am so grateful that you joined us. The weight of the toxicity is so much lighter. I really appreciate your support."

Calvin thought to himself, *She's thanking me for helping me to be a better leader? Not too long ago, I would have seen this kind of thing as a weakness. These two, however, are anything but weak!*

Gertrude continued, "You both seem to be getting the self-authoring and state management shift. Who would have even expected this level of improvement, already?! This is so outside the slam-it-to-the-wall business mentality. This feels sustainable. We are building a new foundation, so we can actually be agile and responsive. I am really excited to see this being integrated into our daily work."

"So, tell me about your silence practice?" Laura asked.

Bob jumped in. "I love Centering Prayer! It fits me better than meditation. I sit and surrender each thought to God. I am even pretty good at holding my attention. I want to work up to two sits a day. Coming home from work less stressed and angry has helped my ability to sit quietly. I had tried before, but I couldn't do it. The coherence training before the silence was a great idea. Thanks for that."

"I am using a more Buddhist-like practice," Calvin shared. "My wife is doing it with me. We bought an online meditation course and are doing it together. We are getting pretty good. We are doing it daily and are up to about twenty minutes a day."

Nine months had passed since the ladies had created a new intention, and PanAm was becoming a different organization. Quite a few people knew they were all working together but so far, no major sabotage. The guys had begun to manage their internal state. In working from Wholeness, they were giving up the blame game, owning what was going on inside themselves first.

The best part was that this new way of being was easy from a calm state. The new responses emerged out of their new perspective and coherence. They didn't have to memorize a playbook. It wasn't behavior modification; it was resetting their physiology—calming their autonomic nervous system—and expanding perception.

"Sounds like you guys are ready to move forward," Gertrude suggested. "We'll put together an outline of the next steps."

"Dialogue builds on all we learned so far, adding greater mindfulness into our conversations," Laura added.

Bob walked out of the meeting with a smile on his face. He was trying not to be too happy, as he had been disappointed before. This seemed like the real deal. If the Dialogue training was as good as what he had learned so far, he was going to be really excited.

The ladies left the office a bit early, getting DB to the park before dark. The sun was just beginning to set and there was a hint of winter in the air. Gertrude felt even more connected to Undivided Wholeness. After a few minutes, the ladies quieted. The silence grew like a living presence. Gertrude could see the shimmering light as she entered the forest. The light expanded into bands of gold and silver weaving between them as they walked. she felt deep-seated love and peace. She perceived the light as beginning to expand into colors. Joy showed as striations of clear yellow. Peace was a beautiful periwinkle blue. *So beautiful.* The ladies walked quietly, both fully aware of Wholeness.

Back at Gertrude's, the two made dinner together. Laura laughed and said, "I love that we can actually leave work early, take a walk, and I feel no guilt. The work is getting done. We will have the outline for the guys in the morning. And we don't have to worry about Tom 'telling on us.' Right there, that emotional dread which no longer exists frees up so much energy! We can take care of ourselves and DB and get it all done."

"Yeah," Gertrude agreed, "that constant low-grade resistance is almost gone. I used to feel a sense of heaviness. Now when it comes back, I notice it and let it go much quicker. I have been carrying some of this around for decades. It's been sucking my energy for years."

As Laura and Gertrude began to eat, a familiar voice joins their conversation.

"It doesn't have to be this way," DB jumped in. "The ancient definition of *Dialogue*—from the roots *dia* and *logos*—is 'flow of meaning.'"

Gertrude began to laugh at the look on Laura's face. She was still not used to DB talking. Laura smiled and shook her head as DB continued.

"At its essence, Dialogue is a discovery process. It respectfully explores what a person believes, how broader worldviews shape opinions and the attachments individuals have to those opinions. At its core, the practice of Dialogue brings people together to learn about individual perceptions and their sources, expanding understanding by being given the opportunity to see through the lens of other people's opinions. In everyday life, true Dialogue is uncommon but not difficult to learn. You are both doing so well with your practice, making it accessible to the guys.

"In learning about and practicing the principles that underpin Dialogue, mutual understanding can be achieved, new common ground can be discovered, new perspectives gained, and bonds between people strengthened. And the two of you already practice moving into stillness. You slow things down, moving out of reaction. That is really great!"

"Thanks, DB, we love you too," Gertrude bent down to love on her fur baby.

DB continued. "Here are the four most fundamental principles of Dialogue:

- Listen with the intent to fully understand.
- Slow things down to make room for silence.
- Notice your assumptions while suspending judgment.
- Before you speak, ask yourself three questions.
    - Have I truly heard what's been said?
    - Is it my turn to speak?
    - Is what I will share in service to the Whole?"

Laura jumped in, "This is a great summary of the principles of Dialogue. Through all of my reading, I found the full version, but this seems like a great place to start."

"Yes," DB continued. "You can see how Dialogue builds on all the intrapersonal work you have already been doing.

"Let's start with: Listen with the intent to fully understand. Most humans think they know how to listen. But, they don't. Growing up, you are told to listen but rarely if ever are taught *how*.

"Listening on the other hand doesn't 'simply happen'; it is something you consciously choose to do. It requires intention. It necessitates concentration. It demands attention.

"Have either of you ever been in a meeting where someone is speaking and you're forming the answer in your head even before the person stops talking?"

"I know Tom has!" Laura interrupts. "Alright... I know... I do it too."

DB continued. "Well, the principle of listening with the intent to fully understand helps you to become more aware of when you are doing just that and more! When you actively participate in listening, you are more present, paying undivided attention, seeking to understand, suspending assumptions, keeping an open mind, and allowing for silence. Which leads me to the next principle: Slow things down to make room for silence."

"I like this one," Gertrude added. "This has been the biggest lifesaver for me over the last few months."

DB inquired, "Did you ever notice that the words *LISTEN* and *SILENT contain* the same letters?" Winking at Gertrude, he went on, "Don't think that's a coincidence. I don't think anything is a coincidence... but that's a story for another time."

Gertrude smiled.

"Most of us are uncomfortable with silence—especially in business. We tend to want to fill any quiet moment with noise," said Laura. "Gertrude, remember those earlier days at the park where we met? It took you some time before you could fully settle into silence. Yet we all know that silence is where real change occurs. In silence, we dissolve the barriers that exist between us. And not just between people, but between us and anything. Gertrude, recall one of your days at the park where you felt at one with the nature that surrounded you. That can only come with silence."

Gertrude, "Yes, it was so beautiful."

"In the practice of Dialogue, people need to intentionally slow things down to make room for silence," said DB. "Embracing silence creates a space to more deeply connect with yourselves, with your surroundings and with others. Letting silence exist between your mental and verbal exchanges allows you to derive meaning from what has been shared, integrating it into your hearts. It is from that place of depth you can become more deeply authentic. With authenticity, there is vulnerability and a dissolution of your self-impose boundaries. People create barriers between each other by their fragmentary thoughts. Each one operates separately. So, when these barriers have dissolved, then there arises one mind, where everyone is all one unit, while each person also retains his or her own individual awareness. It's what I refer to as a *single intelligence*."

"Hold on," Gertrude stopped DB, "I have heard of that; it's also called Unitive Thought, or even enlightenment."

"Wow! Could you imagine what it would be like for our leadership team to operate as a single unit? Even if we only got halfway down that road, it would be amazing. Think of how much we could accomplish if we felt safe and Whole instead of fearful and fragmented. What is the next principle, DB?" Laura asked.

DB replied, "The next principle is to notice your assumptions while suspending opinion. Dialogue is the practice of understanding the attachments you have to your assumptions and how those beliefs shape you, your businesses, and your lives. It involves sharing your opinions, suspending judgment of others' views, and in that, creating meaning through words. It is not part of Dialogue to persuade others that any one opinion is right. At the same time, this does not mean that you cannot have strong opinions when participating in Dialogue."

"Okay, let's slow things down." Laura smiled and said, "Suspending is assuming that my idea is not the only one. I pause and listen and allow, even when the other's idea is different."

"Okay, yeah, but remember this is all part of our intention toward Wholeness," Gertrude shared. "This is how we can take it out into the group, not just inside us. So, the internal process that helped us be so much happier and peaceful is similar to this process we use in conversation. I like how it is all fitting together."

"Yes, that is right," DB continued. "Yet what I mean by suspend is to hang. By suspending your judgments—hanging them out in front so you and others can see and experience them—you can more fully understand one another and from that understanding, derive meaning. Because at the end of the day, the meaning is the 'glue' or 'cement' that holds people and societies together."

"Wait," Gertrude interrupted, "doesn't expressing our judgments create debate and conflict? I mean, what if my view is diametrically opposed to yours?"

"Yes, Gertrude, that's an excellent question!" DB continued. "Defending your views and opinions actually blocks your sensitivity to meaning. Put another way, the biggest thing that gets in the way of Dialogue is holding on to your assumptions, judgments, and opinions and defending them. It is when you become attached to these ideas that you become personally identified with them. This is true for the collective as well. Similar to group think, identifying collectively with a certain mindset or opinion not only sabotages collaboration, but it also creates an environment where people cannot authentically listen and lead."

"When you are attached to a certain assumption or hold a fixed mindset and defend it, the main difficulty is that you cannot listen properly to somebody else's opinion because you are resisting it. People don't really want to hear it, and so, they shut down, creating those barriers between each other."

"So, this is another way to release our resistance," Gertrude interjected. "Laura and I were just talking about how much better I feel not to resist all the time. So, in effect, this is what Tom is doing when his answer is the only correct answer and his outbursts keep people from challenging him. And when Tom does that, he is shutting out other views, minimalizing the intelligence that can come from the group."

"That's good Gertrude. It also reminds me that we are still doing that too. Maybe not as loud, but we lock down, too," Laura said.

"Exactly," DB continued, "and let's be careful here, because everyone defends at some point. Dialogue is therefore not suggesting that it is wrong or bad when you defend. Everyone judges. You all have biases. The practice of Dialogue therefore does not suggest that you judge yourself for defending your opinion; it's rather about noticing when you are defending. Because everyone will defend. Everyone will judge. You will have your biases—it's the brain's way of protecting itself."

"So, this is like not judging our silence practice," Laura added. "To know it is valuable even when I am restless through the whole sit. We keep showing up, we keep practicing, and we allow the practice to change us."

"Yes," DB continued, "the practice is to be sensitive to that which condemns and judges, looking at all the opinions and assumptions and letting them surface. Because assumptions are powerful and people are not usually aware of them. And again—because this is significant—by suspending your assumptions—hanging them out in front so you and others can see and experience them—you can more fully understand one another and from that deeper understanding, derive shared meaning—the bond that profoundly connects people. If I had to sum up the practice of Dialogue in just one word, it would be mindfulness."

"This is great. I like it. It is a clear plan to expand what we have already started," Laura said.

DB continued, "Which leads me to the next and final key principle: Before you speak, ask yourself three questions:

- ❖ Have I heard what's been said?
- ❖ Is it my turn to speak?
- ❖ Is what I will say in service to the Whole?

"Have I heard what's been said? In other words, have you listened with the intent to understand, noticing mental and verbal interruptions, seeing others as 'legitimate' others?

"Is it my turn to speak? Or do you just feel uncomfortable with the silence and want to fill that void with noise?

"Is what I will say in service to the Whole? Or do I just want to hear myself talk because I know the answer; and I have the solution; and I'm trying to fulfill my personal agenda?"

The lesson ended and Gertrude and Laura cleaned up from dinner. DB curled up in his spot on the ottoman. They all relaxed into a blissful reverie.

There was a clarity and presence about Laura and Gertrude. They were grounded and open. It felt good. Laura broke the silence. "I am actually beginning to really see how this all works. And there is no sense of 'I have to make this happen.' We are doing it now. We don't have to push, just keep showing up, growing up and waking up, allowing Wholeness to emerge and lead us."

"Yeah," Gertrude agreed. "I am amazed and feel so blessed."

Chapter 14

It was Monday morning and Bob stomped into his office. He was still angry. He had a big blowup with his ex-wife over the weekend. Things had been going so well for weeks and now he was all the way back at the beginning: angry, tense, and wanting to shut down any bullshit. He was struggling to keep his temper in check and his mind from running. He could easily go off at any moment.

He realized it was probably anger at his ex-wife that was bleeding out. He knew yelling wasn't right, but he couldn't quite pull it back. He stopped for a minute. He knew this was his old self. He had worked like this for years. He also knew that just last Friday, he had consciously been in a different place. There was something he could do, a shift he could make to get back to clarity. *Okay, right now, my practice isn't quite strong enough to break through, but I know someone who can help,* Bob thought to himself. *Time to go talk to Gertrude. Hold on! I am asking for help!?! I am asking a woman who is effectively below me in this organization; and yet, it's completely reasonable. She has the ability to help me cut through all of this.*

I am strongly committed to our intention. I see how it aligns different aspects of my life, and I want it to keep happening. Maybe I have learned something after all. I think this is what the ladies have called growing up. Bob chuckled to himself as he walked down the hall.

Bob found Gertrude in the art department working with her staff. When she saw him, she stepped away and they walked into her private office. "So, what's up? You don't look so good," she started as she shut the door.

"No, I am not, and you look completely at peace. I can feel it coming off of you in waves. It's nice just to be around you." Bob took a deep breath. "The issue is my ex-wife. We had a fight."

"Okay, so your issue is your reaction to your ex-wife—that I can help you with."

"Sure, sure, Thanks, Dr. Gertrude."

Gertrude laughed, and so did Bob. The tension was already breaking up.

They spent a few minutes in silence before beginning. Gertrude listened to Bob's struggle. She could see how his anger had shut him down. She focused on helping him suspend his assumptions and come back into balance. In the end, Gertrude suggested he create a simple phrase to use with his HeartMath practice throughout each day. The repetition of a meaningful phrase deepened a more peaceful response within his nervous system. Especially, if it was something he held deeply.

"I surrender into divine Wholeness" was what he chose. It reminded him a bit of his childhood, when his mom would share with him the goodness in the world, if he only had eyes to see. His experience with religion as a child was loving. But the church he attended when he was married was caustic. He stopped going. Now he was back, attending a church a friend had recommended.

The Centering Prayer group he found there felt right. It seemed to be adding to the good parts of his past religious experiences. He could do this practice privately. He wasn't converting anyone, just using his own memory of presence or Love, as Laura called it, to expand his leadership.

Bob was beginning to remember how he had led in the past. They were not his best moments. He was actually embarrassed and ashamed by some of his behavior. He had learned that this is part of the process—to become more self-aware, looking at his patterns without falling into shame and guilt.

It was a challenge to see how his anger had impacted his employees. He was learning to forgive himself, allowing, accepting, listening, and apologizing where he could. Humanness is expected and normal, but modification needed to happen. This new realization that it is okay to not know an answer and that it is okay to ask for help was profound for Bob. So simple and so scary.

Bob also knew he had stuff hanging around from his divorce. *Maybe I should go to a therapist and get this all out. Gertrude can only help so much,* he thought.

Before the next training session, the ladies emailed their outline on Dialogue. This time, the guys actually read it before the meeting. Yes, things were definitely changing!

Laura began the meeting with a few moments of silence. Then she said, "The best example I have of Dialogue is in these sessions. We listen to understand. We have a moment of silence and slow things down. We watch our judgments and assumptions and we check ourselves before we speak. So really how do we strengthen this more consciously and take it into our workday and life?"

Bob watched as Gertrude and Laura ran the session. They were so great at supporting this process, organized and clear. He knew putting this all together had been a job. He couldn't remember ever having this anywhere before. No one was defending or on some ego rant. It felt strange. He wanted to come, learn, and participate. He felt respected and heard. Sadly, he didn't even have this in his marriage.

Bob loved that he could be himself and fully participate. He didn't have to do the same practice as everyone else, and no one was trying to change him. It required his willingness to grow up and show up better. There was no force. We start where we are. *I love this! Where else could I start?* Bob thought as he laughed to himself.

"Do you have any questions, Bob?" Laura asked.

"No, I'm good. Thanks, Laura and Gertrude; great work here. I really appreciate your professionalism and the kindness. I have never worked like this before. Even with a few bad days, my own productivity is skyrocketing, also!"

"I'm loving this too," Calvin exclaimed. "I'm all in! I've already seen the impact here and at home. Bless your hearts!"

As Bob walked back to his office, he realized he actually felt joy—right now. He also knew how much this was helping him resolve his anger. Anger that until a few months ago, he hadn't even known was there. Bob could see how his old patterns to fight and defend were locked up in his body; how out of balance he had become. *I always thought plowing through life was normal.* Bob laughed to himself. *It was normal! Because I didn't know any other way.*

The four had taken simple practices of mindfulness, silence, and value-based leadership, and began to work from holographic leadership. It was changing his world. Bob's reduced stress and irritability were changing the conversations with his kids and ex-wife. Before all this, he would have held on to his anger for a long, long time. It was such a big difference. He already knew how this would have changed his marriage.

Chapter 15

It had now been a year since Gertrude and Laura started consciously working from Wholeness. Bob and Calvin were fully engaged and involved and Wholeness flowed. Synchronicity and laughter were now a regular part of work. With the daily choice to work from intention and appreciation, significant changes had occurred in the ability to respond to the onslaught of events. Creativity and reality testing had expanded, each knowing Wholeness in his and her own way, allowing it to lead behavior and interactions. The process of clarifying goals and working a plan remained part of the new culture. And even better than before, goals were discussed and agreed upon.

The culture had shifted so much that Tom eventually put in his notice. Over time, his outbursts were no longer tolerated and accountability was immediate. Tom had been offered coaching but chose not to adapt his behavior to the new culture. He didn't get on the bus. The new sales director would be chosen from a different set of criteria, based on a value-based culture of respect.

Laura and Gertrude were driving to lunch. They managed to do this now a couple times a week. It was a great way to break the frantic activity, still hanging around from the old system. "Looking back, it all makes so much sense. Thank God! We found our way through," Laura exclaimed. "It's like we've been pulled into a new future. I feel so incredibly grateful!"

Gertrude and Laura had learned that trying to figure everything out in their heads alone results in a lot of incoherent mental pushing and pulling. Creating a joint venture between their hearts and their minds created alignment and put power behind their goals. They remained grounded and centered through their practice and, of course, their walks with DB. Harnessing the power of coherence gave them the energy needed to achieve in ways that had not been possible before.

The guys joined them for lunch, laughing and enjoying each other's company. "I have an announcement," Bob said. "I am off my blood pressure meds. My doctor was a bit shocked when I told her about my practice. But she agreed it could have this effect. I feel so much better! Wow, who knew the best medical advice I would ever receive would come from my creative director?"

Gertrude smiled. "It's not crazy that the same thing that creates a healthy culture also make us heathier. I too have so much more energy, that constant drag is gone. So much has changed."

"Yes, work flows so much better," Laura added. "This year when I go on vacation, I won't be completely exhausted when I get there."

"I love how the leadership meetings are finally productive. The problem solving is my favorite," Calvin interjected.

After lunch, Gertrude went about her day feeling energized and happy. She stayed focused by seeing her contribution to the Whole, her purpose and sense of belonging. She used her practice to break the old patterns as they occurred, releasing her spinning thoughts. She still fell back into the nonsense from time to time, but the energy suck was so much shorter now.

After work, the ladies drove back to Gertrude's house and took DB for a walk in the forest. They had done this so many times, it was like returning to a warm embrace. The presence of peace immediately filled them; it was their touchstone to joy along with the deep self-care that had allowed the transformation from within.

The women were quiet, grounded, and centered as they walked down the path. They dropped into their normal rhythm, any need for conversation was gone.

Laura was open and relaxed, even more than last year, on the beach. She felt a sense of spaciousness that she hadn't known existed. There were still problems, but not a sense of overwhelm. She was so much less reactive, able to see more clearly, more fully aware of what was true in each moment. Clarity! "You know, Gertrude," she said, "I didn't realize how strong clarity makes me feel. There is an assurance that I will be able to see and figure out the problems, real confidence! I really like it!"

Gertrude smiled.

Laura and Gertrude had worked from a clear vision and then brought the ideas into reality through logic, insight, and intuition. They developed the ability to step back from the surface tension and see the patterns within the Whole, the details within the tasks. Laura loved this fluid, spacious state. This was the transformation they had longed for; it was now a reality. She knew there would be challenges as this work expanded deeper into PanAm. But they knew how to hold their vision and remain centered. The process would continue, step by step. The momentum was palpable.

The guys where fully onboard and holding the intention and values along with them. The path forward had not yet fully emerged, but it would. They were a synchronized team: honest, direct, and clear. Differences were heard. There was no need for any of the old games and no desire to defend. With a shared sense of meaning, all of them knew how to center and see the opportunities within the moment and lead toward them. Without understanding interconnection, this would all sound crazy.

Gertrude was lost in the beauty as it had been the night of her initial vision. She could see the luminous light with its shimmers of color weaving into Wholeness. There was a gentleness that was present.

Gertrude felt the clarity too. *It's all right here. The necessary pause so critical to knowing the immense courageous gentleness—a moment of being grounded and centered that allows for ideas and insight to emerge. I simply allow it to be and pay attention*, she mused.

The forest radiated light as the women continued deeper into the forest.

DB broke the silence, "The universe is not separate from this cosmic sea of energy. Our consciousness is more than our awareness and attention."

"We are all One," Gertrude whispered.

"Yes," DB whispered back. "Yes."

Laura and Gertrude continued down the path into the forest taking in the beauty and light. "Hey, Gertrude, why don't you use your middle name, Marie? It has such color and light."

Gertrude smiled. "I love that idea! I do feel like a new person. It's a great way to mark this new way of being. Yes! From now on I am Marie."

After walking in the park, Marie could still feel a tingle through her body, a Presence. She could feel Wholeness, its lightness and joy. She moved slowly around her home, savoring the Love and an expanded sense of self. She remembered that Friday evening a year ago, sitting on a log completely overwhelmed.

In her own way, Marie knew she had been praying for a miracle that night. DB was such an unexpected synchronicity and yet there is no doubt he was drawn into her life by Love. How could any rational, analytical solution ever come up with adding a dog to her life? It had nothing to do with the problem. Did it? Wholeness has a way of connecting, allowing synchronicities with things that appear unconnected.

It was exactly the change in momentum and direction she needed. *Thank God for Wholeness!!!* Marie said to DB, with that oxymoron she laid back on the bed, laughing. DB was right there, licking her face and getting in on the loving.

Marie went to bed that night feeling deeply connected to Wholeness. DB snuggled in close. They both fell into a deep sleep. And in this sleep, Marie dreamed.

In the dream she heard the voice of wisdom—*The universe is Love. At our birth, we are given a prepared canvas on which to paint our dreams, our world. We color our world based on the emotional frequencies we choose. We paint our world first in the colors our parents taught us. We can paint our whole lives in dark sullen colors and feel oppressed, or we can paint our lives in the most beautiful rainbow of colors—yellows, purples, reds and blues—blessed by the joy of their presence. It is these very choices that shape our world.*

Many of us choose to surround ourselves with others who see the world through the same lens, and paint from the same palette. This allows us to affirm that what we have chosen is right. Of course, our choice is always right, as we are free to choose any color, any frequency, and any emotion.

We get to choose, "Is this the color? Is this the frequency? Is this the life I want?"

Too often, we are strongly attached to what we know. Unaware, we reinforce our choices. By releasing our attachment to our emotions—to the meaning we have placed on the things and events around us—we are free to recognize the perfection of what is and we are free to create a world we would like to see right here, right now. To see the Love that stands behind All That Is is the freedom we seek. Love provides us the power from which to draw on our canvas of life. It is here we become artists of color and light.

Marie woke up with a profound sense of bliss. She felt how deeply she had accepted her power. Now she understood how true power comes from one's internal capacities and seeing the Wholeness of all that exists. There is no separation between ideas and intent, so the Wholeness that is the universe is brought forth with the intention of positive change. But without recognizing the entire process, from ideas to intent to action, and the Wholeness involved, the energy dynamic is often cut off.

Marie now realized all of this and felt blessed, for now she knew how to see the truth of what it means to release doubt in herself and her place in the world. To walk a path of beauty. Not from a place of **Happily Ever After** or even **The End** but instead, a new beginning and deeper trajectory into the never-ending journey of Undivided Wholeness.

The Beginning . . .

Part Two

*Living into Wholeness:
The Journey*

Introduction

A Call to Wholeness offers an expanded way of being to help us be change agents in our world. It does not follow the greed model of business that is so rampant. It moves out of the illusion that doing good works is enough and has us digging deeper into our own shadow and prejudice so that we can minimize the outward projection of our own imperfections.

We are always in the process of becoming. *A Call to Wholeness* offers an opportunity to deepen our own development. We have enough toxic waste in this world; let's stop further polluting it through our words, behavior, and actions.

Integrated within this fairy tale is the literature from many fields of study. The audience for this book is educated and has read many business and leadership books already. If intellectual knowledge was all that was needed, we would have gained clarity and coherence already. So, what are the elusive pieces?

Our story brings leadership up to date into a world where everything is energy. The transition to this worldview will disrupt the current balance of individual and organizational leadership. By integrating the quantum world, a nonlinear model of reality is introduced. Nonlinear includes nonanalytical ways of knowing. It changes the power dynamics, moving away from the traditional hierarchical, top-down format to an interconnected net of influence. It moves beyond our left-brain and the use of force into the Whole of us: heart, mind, and body. As we lead from Wholeness, we lead from all of who we are, and together, we can create a Whole world.

Our story looks at the world of business from a view of the new science, Undivided Wholeness in flowing movement. For us, this means deep interconnection. This nonlinear world is where the unseen is the primary influencer, and the smaller is more powerful. Wholeness offers a completely different view of leadership and organizational change. It changes the rules and what we know of leadership. This shift begins within the leader—her psychological and physiological functioning—and then moves into the organization, the group's field dynamics. In our story, the ladies began their development internally and then impacted the organization.

The journey deeper into Wholeness begins within each of us. To even hear the call, to follow the longing, we need to realize the importance of self-care. Most of us are so fragmented we don't even know we are exhausted, having no energy or attention for one more thing. That is why our story is a fairy tale meant to entertain and seed possibility.

Part Two takes the whimsy of our story and moves it into everyday practice, gathering the literature and theories discussed and bringing them back into the left brain for understanding and application.

The first section is on "Overall Wellbeing." Here is where we explore self-care and offer a path to clarity, coherence, and peace. Through a self-learning process, Marie (formally known as Gertrude) and Laura retrained themselves to remember their interconnectedness from moment to moment. The journey began by shifting their physical state to increase their conscious awareness and psychological development. It began from a sense of overwhelm and a need to deal with the toxic stress and their experience of something bigger than themselves.

The capacity for self-care is the basis of our ability to be leaders. Emotional intelligence, reality testing, clear critical thinking, active self-awareness, and interpersonal relationships—these skills become our core strength, the muscle that supports our leadership. This clarity moves out into our organizations, building a strong, robust, and caring culture. The literature is clear on the critical importance of these "softer" skills.

When we are overworked, overwhelmed, exhausted, and irritable, we fall back into the get-it-done, slam-it-through style of leadership. After all, it is how we were taught. We know the slang term for hardworking is *head down*. Many will still consider this to be an absolute reality. But this is not in our best interest and it doesn't bring the best results. We don't even realize how cut off we are from our insight and intuition and then wonder why we aren't more agile and creative.

Coming into an internal coherent state is critical for any change process, be it individual or organizational. Without this foundational shift, we are locked into our old reactions, physically, mentally, spiritually, and emotionally—keeping biochemical reflexes that hold us in fragmentation. Sustainable change does not work from fragmentation. A new culture requires a new way of being, a new way of leading—and it starts with becoming more Whole.

In our fairy tale, we watched the ladies move away from reactivity and learn to really listen. This alone was enough to begin a shift in their departments. We watched them take responsibility for their reactions and their actions, then accept and release them. Not suppressing or denying them.

As we slow down and become more centered and present, we can turn our attention to our development as leaders—growing up, waking up, and showing up in ways that are fundamental to maturity and success. In doing this, we become steady enough to lead in ways that are purpose-driven and values-based, developing ourselves into conscious, entrepreneurial, visionary leaders.

Next, in "Holographic Leadership," we discuss the scientific, psychological and leadership literature woven throughout the story, commenting on various aspects of leading purpose-driven organizations and what it means to shift from self-interest to service.

Holographic leadership is a blend of values-based leadership, the understanding of our very real, energetic interconnection and our internal state. It extends out into our organization through conscious self-awareness, increased listening, reduced reactivity, Dialogue, and allowing all voices to be heard.

In holographic leadership, our coherent heart field (think EKG) becomes a point of reference and of synchronization, either cohering or fragmenting the group. This point of reference is true for formal, titled leaders and informal leaders, who hold powerful influence. It recognizes a formal hierarchical organizational structure and builds toward a networked web of interrelationship.

It is our clarity and coherence that allows up to show up and actually lead from our values, vision, and purpose. Without this core strength and coherence, our values become like a plaque on the wall and our limitations get acted out through the organization. Our behavior is the barometer of our values. Regardless of what we say, our behavior expresses our values, so our behavior can be used as a reality check.

In our story, the ladies were able to draw on the unexpressed organizational values and align themselves with a more mindful expression of leadership. They chose their intention and held themselves accountable. They managed their behavior and their thoughts. They were able to recognize "slips" away from their intention and correct. No shame, no blame, no guilt, just awareness and correction. Conscious awareness and adjustment is the ongoing work of holographic leadership.

Marie and Laura worked together to step through their own obstacles. They were open, vulnerable, and psychologically strong enough to look for and find areas within themselves that contributed to the toxicity. Once they were able to see their own reactions and the mental fog, they were free to step out of them. This took time and commitment. From clarity and coherence, they could address obstacles within the organization. Holographic leadership seeks reality. When the actual problem can be seen, it is much more likely to be resolved.

"The success of any intervention is dependent upon the interior condition of the intervenor," says William O'Brien, CEO, Hanover Insurance. We can develop our interiority and our leadership abilities simultaneously, as long as we remember **our inner state is the container that holds our capacity to lead**. It is not an accessory. Our interior state is the foundation of our leadership.

Overall Wellbeing

Marie and Laura used a number of practices to move from overwhelm to clarity. First was physical exercise, walking in this case. Going to the gym, participating in a spin class, or taking a walk at the end of the day can help to clear all the built-up stressors.

But perhaps this is easier said than done. We all know how challenging it can be to do some form of physical exercise, especially at the end of a busy day. Yet physical exercise is such a simple way to burn off the built-up stress chemicals, to reset our body.

Getting up and moving is so important. Make your commitment; find the way that works for you; and maybe ask someone to join you. When walking or running, a simple phrase or "mantra" can support us as a way of keeping our minds from reengaging in all that we experience during the workday.

If you choose to seek out a partner on this journey, remember s/he needs to be someone who supports the agreed upon intention and vision. It is not someone with whom to exchange complaints through some sort of bitch session. It is someone who is dedicated to working from Wholeness, as you support one another to interrupt old patterns when they surface. And they will resurface.

Next, the ladies needed a mindfulness practice they could easily and practically use at work. HeartMath offers an on-demand system. It can be quickly learned and done while walking down the hall or driving your car. Most importantly, it helps speed along the resetting of our autonomic nervous system and biochemistry. This means it releases some of the stress stored in our bodies and interrupts our stress cycle.

Most of us have been taught to go along to get along and to suck it up and move forward when a problem arises. And that can be necessary, at times. Unfortunately, what we haven't been taught is how to release the stressor. We have a lot of old debris—toxicity—built up in our system. The stressors we are carrying become unconscious reflexes in our nervous system. All of this keeps us in hyperdrive, mentally running fast enough to keep the pain away and rendering us unable to be emotionally present. Many—if not most of us— are all but blind to this continuous, automatic internal process.

We can get caught in our reactions, even as we consciously watch them: *Okay, I'm noticing that this is a reaction. It's an old pattern. I know I am triggered. I won't be able to see the opportunity here until I get out of this state.* While it's mindful to notice when we feel triggered, simply being aware of a reaction is not usually sufficient enough to break the reflex. HeartMath gives some easily used tools for this. Our self-awareness helps us remember to use them.

In addition to the HeartMath system, there are many other ways to release our emotional/biochemical reflexes, including emotional freedom technique. EFT or tapping is a technique formulated and tested in the 1980s by Sue Johnson and Les Greenberg. This technique has now grown in popularity and is a growing subject of research. Tapping helps us to shake the small traumas out of our system. Not the memory of what triggers you—just the trigger itself. It's a simple way to learn how to regain clarity in areas where we are normally reactive.

It is this clarity that is critical in leadership. Moving from a reactive state to a more receptive one is significant to our psychological development as leaders. All of our emotional reactions from our lifetime are stored in our nervous system and they can be triggered at any time. Breaking the pattern within our amygdalae—the more primitive, so-called "reptilian" parts of our brain that can lock us into a fight, flight, or freeze reaction—allows us to move forward in ways that are more accepting, creative, and mature.

Further to HeartMath and EFT, qigong, a Chinese practice of physical exercises and breathing control related to tai chi, can also be helpful in releasing triggers—both from the active (the trigger itself) and passive aspect (awareness/emotional management).

For both leadership and real Dialogue, our interior condition must be more centered, calm, and present. It's our hyper-aroused nervous system that directly impairs our ability to engage in clear, critical thinking and deep listening.

Our highest functioning is built on the capacity to expand our perception and move to a more spacious sense of being, actively remembering our interconnection. From a quantum-holographic perspective, **Wholeness is primary. We are not trying to reconnect; we are already connected—there is no separation.** We are expanding our perception to see what is already there. We have been trained to believe that this perception is not real.

In embracing this worldview, we remove the obstacles that block our awareness of Wholeness. We move from a reactive state of mind to a receptive state. Our reactive mind is cluttered and often spinning. A receptive mind sees and responds differently. Our receptive mind is able to listen, allow and accept, holding different points of view and diversity of thought instead of defending them. A receptive mind is generous, kind, and strong and it creates harmony rather than division. Harmony is the very state of being that is Dialogue, a state wherein deeper understanding emerges and higher solutions are born.

The next practice is a game changer—the centering practice we call *silence*. There are so many options here. HeartMath offers a secular exercise. Every major religion has some kind of contemplative practice. Centering Prayer, Buddhist meditation, Transcendental Meditation, or simply sitting in silence as you focus on your breath. Picking a meaningful practice is a great way to deepen a sense of purpose in your work.

We don't recommend you use any kind of practice that offers you a quick fix or a fast track. Not only can it be harmful to you physically, psychologically and neurologically, there's a reason the words *SILENT* and *LISTEN* contain the same letters. And as Laura shared when Calvin asked how long he should sit in silence: "According to the Buddha, one should sit and meditate for twenty minutes each day. Unless you are too busy; then you should sit for two hours."

The point of silence is to *move toward* a state of internal stillness and become aware of our constant, streaming thoughts. Notice we didn't say clear your mind or be completely still. It is a process. It is a practice. Just like cleaning your house or organizing your desk, it requires continual daily attention. It is in the recentering, the intentional adjustment of our focus that flexes the muscle, building the strength for clarity. The training of our focus, the multitude of internal adjustments we make throughout each day, like doing reps at the gym, makes us stronger and clearer. It is a daily choice to manage our internal state, to align with our values, and to act with integrity.

Wholeness is. It is a constant. To know it requires willingness and a shift in our attention and physical state. From a calmer, quieter place, we can begin to know and act from interconnection. **In holographic leadership, attention is our point of power.** Where we place our attention becomes a critical decision. The discipline of maintaining a calm, clear state brings clarity, which allows us to progress toward our goals and align with our purpose and values. **Focus becomes the means of creating and executing goals**.

> *What you choose, with each action and each thought, is an intention, a quality of consciousness that you bring to your action or your thought.*
>
> Gary Zukav

It is our baggage that blocks our progress, the old memories and hurts that get triggered in us. The process of clearing away our stored pain is not fun; it's downright uncomfortable. It is something that most people actively resist. We spend a great deal of energy and attention blocking out painful memories. For the most part this is seen as good and strong. But this pain just comes out sideways and gets spewed all over your organization. With greater self-awareness, it can be managed and even resolved.

Some of us will benefit from a therapist. For others, a coach, mentor, or trusted friend is enough. Either way, the person who is offering you feedback needs to have done their own work. You can only take people to your own level of development. Philosopher Ken Wilber distinguishes between *growing up*—the personal development required of us to lead—and *cleaning up*—the personal healing that often requires assistance. Each of us is on a different journey; it is important to start where we are.

The chart below is a compilation created by Ken Wilber using the various theories of psychological development. They are placed in such a way as to emphasize the similarities between them. Values-based leadership beings at Level 4, formal operational. Holographic leadership begins at the Level 5, high vision-logic. The names are not important, growing up and showing up are.

Jan Byars, PhD & Susan Taylor

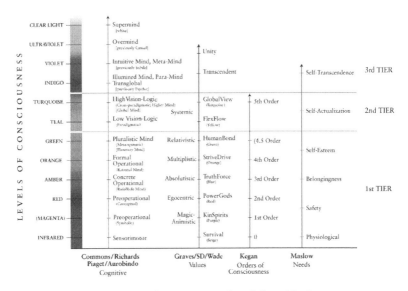

Figure 4.1 from Ken Wilber/Shambhala

It is through our own maturity and internal discipline that we develop the power to hold an environment for growth and innovation and to lead an organization. **Our attention becomes an agent of change.**

The practices used by Marie and Laura show us how to begin to observe our own mind and heart, to remember our Wholeness. **This observation and correction is the journey deeper into Wholeness.** Through this comes the ability to realize that we are not our internal chatter. It becomes easier to suspend our thoughts, to observe and allow. As we become less identified with the rightness of our thoughts and ideas, we can allow others to have a voice, to allow greater diversity and Wholeness to emerge. Our story offers a challenge— an opportunity to integrate and heal more deeply—to lead with greater clarity.

Honoring our feelings as a legitimate aspect of self is embedded throughout all of the practices Laura and Marie used. Being *actively aware of* and managing our mental and emotional state—maintaining our groundedness and centeredness—staying connected to our heart, mind, and body is the core of being a conscious leader. Sometimes this means letting our emotions flow, feeling the pain we have stored. This part is unpleasant and yet important. This healing work is best done with people you trust.

The need for authenticity and vulnerability in our story and in our leadership is clear. It is our self-awareness that is the essence of emotional intelligence and allows us to stay vulnerable and open to possibility. When we can do this, we can access the insight that lies beneath our emotion.

The old system likes to pretend we don't have these kinds of feelings and emotions, even as we see them expressed in our organizations daily. The new system has our interiority at its core—the process of becoming more and more aware of what drives us, enabling us to be able to solve more complex problems.

All of these practices help us to disengage and detach from our running, chattering mind, reducing our reactionary tendencies and triggers. As we move into a receptive state, we lead with our whole self: heart, mind, and body. The resetting of the autonomic nervous system is what helps us hold this shift. This physical shift within is a critical differentiator in organizational change. There are multiple ways to walk this path, pick your starting point, and allow it to build and emerge.

You might be thinking, *I can't do all of that!* And you are right.

Trying to do too much too fast is the quickest path to overwhelm and giving up. Accepting and allowing ourselves to be where we are is an absolute necessary part of this process. We could even say it is the process. **Be aware. Accept your reality. Take whatever steps you**

can, no matter how small, and keep going. This is a continuous process where small, consistent steps create a sustainable path. There is absolutely no need to take a quantum jump off the proverbial cliff. Take your time. Be gentle to yourself. And honor the process as a journey not a sprint—not another race to run.

We don't want to create a sense of urgency. This process is done with commitment, hope, and optimism. It is done with clear, consistent dedication and intention. We can only begin from where we are and then go forward. Presence builds over time.

What can you commit to do, right here, right now?

Holographic Leadership

Holographic Leadership is built on the shoulders of values-based leadership. The shift in the leadership literature began with Robert Greenleaf and James McGregor Burns in the 1970s.

Greenleaf discussed the importance of our interior state and of relating to one another in less coercive, more creative, and supportive ways. Often misunderstood, a servant-leader is actually in service to all stakeholders, creating an organizational culture of service that extends well past its doors—out into the community and the world. But it begins within the leaders and the organization.

The true test for a servant-leader is measured through the development of the individuals within the organization. Do all stakeholders grow as people? Do they become healthier, wiser, freer, and more autonomous? Does the organization have a culture of learning and respect and purpose where employees come together to have a positive impact for the organization and greater good?

> *Simply practice being aware. Look, and be still. Feel, and be still.*
> *Listen, and be still.*
>
> Robert Greenleaf

James Macgregor Burns offered the world transformational leadership. He incorporated concepts such as justice and equality into the field of leadership and objected to the worldview that the end justifies the means. Burns opened possibilities for questioning how a leader's attitudes and behaviors affected the organization, its employees, and their working conditions. Burns suggested leaders can shape, alter, and elevate the motives, values, and goals of followers.

Transformational leadership unites people in the pursuit of higher goals that represents the collective or pooled interests of leaders and followers, *leadership for the common good*. It is from this profound shift that the field of values-based leadership has its roots and continues to grow. Holographic leadership would mean little without this strong base built over fifty years.

Holographic leadership expands these critical shifts and integrates a model of quantum Wholeness. It assumes interconnection as the basis of our physical universe, where the Whole is greater than the sum of the parts. Holographic fields are based on a field concept of order, meaning information of the whole system is enfolded into the implicate field and distributed to all of its parts. More simply put, *holographic* means infinite interconnection, all parts enfolded into the Whole.

Many authors and scientists have delineated interconnection. In our story, we draw from the work of physicist David Bohm and philosopher Pierre Teilhard de Chardin.

Undivided Wholeness in flowing movement was Bohm's first descriptor of what is now called quantum holographic theory. In his seminal work, *Wholeness and the Implicate Order,* Bohm introduced concepts that are now mainstreamed; our deep interconnection, an implicate order which remains unseen, yet real and influences outcomes. Bohm stressed how our own fragmentation impairs our ability to see, think, and understand our world. He refers to this state as *sustained incoherence.*

The power of Bohm's understanding of wholeness and its enfolded order has had a significant impact on science's view of the cosmos and can have an equally significant impact on our lives and our leadership. These ideas have already begun to shape the leadership literature.

Teilhard de Chardin's seminal work, *The Human Phenomena*, describes the development of consciousness from the Big Bang. His work as a paleontologist and priest predates Bohm's work. His understanding integrated evolution and creation, upsetting the Catholic Church which sent him to China for decades. Teilhard saw Love not as emotionality or sentimentality but as a force of Nature. He believed that Love fulfills the physics definition of work; that Love is actually a stronger more active force than the other four: electromagnetism, gravity, and the strong and weak nuclear forces. He saw Love working against entropy. Even at the molecular level it attracts, builds, and unites. Love as a core energy.

> *The physical structure of the universe is love.*
> Pierre Teilhard de Chardin

Both Bohm and Teilhard's work has been considered unorthodox. Their ideas are now being seen in a new light.

It is from these origins that Marie's understanding of Wholeness and Laura's understanding of Love developed. DB shared many significant concepts in his conversations with the ladies. They were drawn directly from Bohm's books *Thought as a System* and *On Dialogue*.

Individually, holographic leadership builds on Wholeness and interconnection, accessed through our heart and the field it generates. A coherent heart (as determined by our heart rate variability) is the physical definition of holding steady. It allows clarity and critical thinking. The vagus nerve is a direct link between our heart and neocortex. Our heart feeds our brain coherence or fragmentation.

Our clear, calm state is our capacity to expand our perception into the implicate order, to sense what is wanting to emerge.

A coherent heart field has specific biomarkers—when our heartbeat is in synchronization with our breath and when the biochemistry produced by the heart strengthens us. A coherent heart field allows us to drop into synchronization with those around us. It is through our individual coherent heart fields that organizations can entrain toward a common good, where energy and attention are seen as vital resources and the health of our people (and planet) are seen as a necessary.

> *The rational calculus model of decision-making and following through pays little attention to the inner state of the decision maker.*
>
> Peter Senge

Holographic leadership deepens values-based leadership by including our psychological and physical state. The clarity generated by holographic leadership increases our awareness of the debilitating effects of anger, fear, greed, and pride. Balancing our incoherent emotions becomes an actual business strategy. A coherent organization becomes a primary aim shifting the holding environment of the organization and the impact of environmental conditions. It changes our capacity to lead.

This shift expands our ability to listen and allow new, quieter voices within the organization to speak. Dialogue becomes possible. Acting from integrity with clear intention, powered by positive emotions becomes one of the most powerful things we can do.

Like values-based leadership, holographic leaders know that holding an environment for productive work is a primary task. The tasks of leadership from out story come from Ronald Heifetz, *Leadership*

Without Easy Answers. His more current work is *The Practice of Adaptive Leadership*.

> *The currency of leadership is attention.*
> *Ronald Heifetz*

Holographic leadership moves beyond the typical understanding of culture, to include an actual interactive, energetic field. One that coheres outcomes and allows what has been called *flow* or *being in the zone*. We learn to watch the actual field patterns and our capacity to synchronize together. We can begin to see patterns within our organizations that clearly either strengthen or interrupt them. The capacity for a pattern to strengthen an organization places a stronger emphasis on mindful self-awareness and authenticity, which become foundational to running the organization.

Holographic leadership accepts the need to identify common values and to hold ourselves accountable for their execution. In both values-based and holographic leadership, the means do not justify the outcome. We give up the Machiavellian goal of looking good in favor of actually striving for the common good. How we lead is as important as what we are producing.

If we are out of coherence, our heart field is out of phase with Undivided Wholeness. It is chaotic and disrupted. The momentum so sought in business is not possible.

Holographic leadership accepts the reality that force creates an equal and opposite reaction. This is so clearly seen in the passive-aggressive behavior within PanAm in the story, which operates from the most common leadership model of command and control. Leading from interconnection changes our focus from greed to the common good.

Marie and Laura began their journey from a values-based perspective that was based on the material drawn from training programs they had attended and books they had read. They were able to overcome their level of overwhelm and the toxicity within PanAm through centering practices and exercise. From this place of increased clarity and coherence they were able to engage a coherent holding environment for their individual departments and move it out into the meetings they attended. And as they engaged with more people, Dialogue was able to emerge.

David Bohm often referred to Dialogue as a stream of meaning. Using the metaphor of a river and its banks, meaning can flow among, through, and between people. The banks represent different opinions, experiences, and points of view. The purpose of Dialogue is not to analyze or advocate and win, or even to exchange opinions, but rather to listen and suspend judgment with an intention to gain new perspective. The collective meaning of the entire group emerges from intentionally holding space for differences. From this collective meaning, this shared significance, new understanding is born—something fresh and completely unintended. Something creative. A novel insight occurs from the very thing that holds people and societies together: shared meaning. By intentionally holding space for differences to be made known, each person is participating in listening for the meaning within the group while also taking part in it. It's in this creative tension that new realities are born.

The practice of Dialogue creates a space where there are no winners or losers, allowing people with diverse perspectives to discuss important and meaningful topics. Dialogue comes from people feeling safe and respected no matter how great their differences. It is possible for people who strongly disagree with one another's views to still have an opportunity to learn from each other without feeling forced to either protect or change their opinions.

Like holographic leadership, Dialogue has the potential to create a space for psychological safety—where all stakeholders can authentically show up, participating without fear of negative consequences to self-image, position, or career. This psychological safety is essential to the holding environment of holographic leadership. In short, psychological safety begins with the inner state of the leaders. When present, safety allows the elements necessary for creativity and innovation to appear within a group.

How do you create safety in teams? Through listening. And suspending our preconceived ideas. David Bohm suggests that if people could listen to one another in a way that encouraged all opinions to be heard—*without defending ideas as right or wrong*—business and society would work differently for the betterment of everyone.

Holographic leaders absolutely understand the significance of participatory listening. Theirs is a perspective that involves creating an opportunity to listen while gently noticing our inner reactions and thoughts. Listening with the intent to fully understand another's view gives us the power to come together in a harmonious field.

An obstacle to Dialogue comes when we cling to our assumptions, judgments, and opinions and defend them. When we become attached to ideas that we become identified with, we view that as an attack on ourselves. This is true for us individually and collectively. Identifying with a certain mindset or opinion not only sabotages collaboration, but it also creates an environment where people cannot authentically listen and lead. Similar to group think, when you are attached to a certain assumption or hold a fixed mindset *and defend it,* you cannot listen properly to someone else's opinion. We don't really want to hear it, so we shut down, creating barriers between us.

When we defend, we divide. When we hold steady, we create harmony.

But we are human. We will defend. We will judge. We will have our biases. Dialogue is therefore not suggesting that you judge yourself for defending your opinion but simply notice it. The practice is to be sensitive to that which condemns and judges, letting assumptions come to the surface. Assumptions are so very powerful because we are not usually aware of them. By suspending our assumptions, opinions, and points of view—hanging them out in front of us so we and others can see and experience them—we can more fully understand one another. From that deeper understanding, we derive shared meaning. This deeply bonds us.

As its essence, Dialogue is a practice that helps us to consciously nurture our state of being. And it can be challenging to manage, especially in toxic environments. This is why silence and mindfulness are so critical and a requisite for holographic leaders.

In today's turbulent business environment, leaders must address challenges and opportunities from several perspectives at once. The principles of Dialogue become helpful here, as they require us to slow down and become silent. Without silence, we cannot truly listen. When we cannot listen, we automatically defend.

Dialogue requires us to be mindful of what is happening within as we communicate with others. Through silence and mindfulness, our exchanges with others become holographic: paying attention to our inner state while at the same time being consciously present to the Whole.

Holographic leadership offers a potential for a transformational shift into a more coherent, stable culture. The ladies brought awareness to their intention and then operated from it. They did not go around pretending all was well. They learned to stop projecting their own issues onto the organization. They began to see which part of the issues resided within them and which were in the environment. They actively pursued balance. They listened and accepted other people's views.

Laura and Marie were able to use their intrapersonal strength to have tough conversations, because they were willing to see what was happening and respond in a way that increased their health and that of the organization. When we understand our impact, we can more clearly see the system and leverage its critical points.

Holographic leadership functions in full reality testing. Like all organizations, goals and key performance indicators are relevant. There will be threats and obstacles. From a place of clarity, we scan for all of what is happening both in the environment and within ourselves. The issues are noted and managed. We focus on possibility, we capture opportunity, and we manage threats. We are able to respond with greater accuracy, speed, and agility.

We now have the opportunity to consciously create a culture of creativity and innovation. It is clarity and calmness that allows insight and intuition to be an integral part of our leadership. Holographic leadership is a model of acceptance, appreciation, and reality testing.

How do we attempt this? Through silence. Through listening. Through staying grounded in the moment, aligning heart, mind, and body. And—similar to Laura and Marie—through discovering and committing to various tools and practices that help us to slow down the process of thought and increase our awareness of possibility.

And yet—even with these well documented skills—when it comes to the intensity within business dynamics, we tend to forget that *everything is energy*, often moving us back into the Newtonian mindset of linearity and separateness. We use force in our organizations and then pretend there is not an equal and opposite reaction coming. We turn a blind eye to the toxicity and passive-aggressive behavior. We are told to toughen up. This ends up translating to a complete lack of engagement.

There is another way. Our understanding of the universe has shifted, even if we pretend it hasn't. Everything is energy, really, not just electronics and phones and games. We are no longer limited to the separateness and intellectualism of the Enlightenment that came about in the seventeenth century. Our understanding has significantly grown in the last 300 years; it's now based on the holographic organization of the universe. We use fields in all areas of our lives, yet many leaders still insist on—and even fight for—a worldview that is over three centuries out of date.

It is this expanded sense of our interrelationship that the ladies took into business. It was a process—an experiment even—requiring some trial and error to find their way. And as with all developmental processes, it took time. It did not negate their previous understanding of the Newtonian world. It did not require the ladies to forget all they knew or release all their anger. Their understanding and their practice evolved, transcending, and encompassing the older ideas.

A conscious, purpose-driven organization is held through values-based leadership expanded into holographic leadership. The ongoing process is one of increasing our awareness and realigning ourselves toward our vision and values along with the willingness to look at our own impact within the organization, including the very real possibility that we are the primary obstacle.

Holographic leadership has us consciously create our organizations. Through coherent conditions, we synchronize and draw forth a transformational shift for ourselves, our employees, and our organizations. We need strength to overcome 300-year-old views. We need commitment to more fully understand how our organizations affect our communities. Our own internal state is now the *necessary* foundation, the primary container for our leadership.

This new way of being has us suspend and allow—the opposite of the perfectionistic, hardened persona, driving an outcome through at all costs. Holographic leadership stands in sharp contrast to the command and control model of leadership still so widely used today. It changes the responsibilities we hold for ourselves, our teams, our communities, our environment, and our world.

Appendix A: Resources

The resources listed here supply background and helpful insight to how we can mature as leaders. Our leadership very much lives in our capacity to grow past our limitations. The resources below are some of our favorites and are only a fraction of what is available.

Overall Wellbeing

We start with self-regulation. It can be challenging to sit in silence or have clarity without some degree of calm. Self-regulation is a critical starting point for the type of leadership we describe in this book.

A mindfulness practice that you can take to work is critical. HeartMath offers a system of techniques that can be easily used while walking down the hall. Coaches are available through their website at HeartMath.com

The HeartMath Solution: The HeartMath Institute's Revolutionary Program for Engaging the Power of the Heart's Intelligence (HarperOne; 1st edition, April 7, 1999) by Doc Childre teaches simple ways we can bring ourselves into coherence. This is the same coherence that David Bohm discussed as being vital for clarity of thought and our ability to problem solve the biggest issues of our time.

Heart Intelligence: Connecting with the Intuitive Guidance of the Heart, (Waterfront Digital Press February 13, 2016) by the

HeartMath Institute lays out how intuition and our own inner knowing can be cultivated through coherence. It focuses on care and concern for people much like servant leadership.

Emotional Freedom Technique (EFT) or ***Tapping*** offers another way to break the hold our biochemical reflexes have on us. There are many providers and YouTube videos available. EFT is not quite as on-demand as using the HeartMath system, but it can be helpful when we get really churned up and can't break out of the emotion.

Integral Meditation: Mindfulness as a Path to Grow Up, Wake Up, and Show Up in Your Life, (Shambhala; Illustrated edition, March 15, 2016) by Ken Wilber delineates the stages of psychological development and levels of consciousness talked about in our story. It suggests ways to integrate them into our lives.

Immunity to Change: How to Overcome It and Unlock the Potential in Yourself and Your Organization, Leadership for the Common Good (Harvard Business School Press; 1st edition February 1, 2009) by Robert Kegan discusses the same aspect of our development as Wilber's work though it offers a more psychological view.

Brené Brown has written a great deal on how to own our pain and limitations, and she has brought this into our work. Both of the following books offer great understanding of the impact of our emotions on those we lead. ***Daring Greatly: How the Courage to be Vulnerable Transforms the Way We Live, Love, Parent and Lead*** (Avery; Reprint edition, April 7, 2015) and ***Dare to Lead: Brave Work. Tough Conversations. Whole Hearts*** (Random House; First Edition, October 9, 2018).

Falling Upward: A Spirituality for the Two Halves of Life (Jossey-Bass, 1st edition, April 19, 2011) by Richard Rohr blends Jungian psychology with spiritual formation, focusing on our development in the second half of life.

Seat of the Soul (Simon & Schuster; Anniversary edition, March 11, 2014) by Gary Zukav shows us the critical importance of attention and intention from a view of Wholeness, based in science and his understanding of Source.

Heartfulness (School of Spiritual Psychology, March 1, 2017) by Robert Sardello reveals the mystery of heart-awareness. These practices bring about the capacity to open-hearted awareness as our spiritual organ of deep presence—to ourselves, to others, to the world, and to the Earth.

Wild Mercy: Living the Fierce and Tender Wisdom of the Woman Mystics (Sounds True, April 2, 2019) by Mirabai Starr offers a view of wisdom from many religious perspectives.

This final group of resources offers different silence practices from various perspectives. There are so many others. Find the one that is meaningful for you.

Cynthia Bourgeault, ***The Heart of Centering Prayer*** (Shambhala, December 27, 2016). Centering Prayer is Christian-based silence practice that has us surrender to the presence and action of God.

Pema Chödrön, ***Start Where You Are*** (TarcherPerigee, August 11, 2015) is an interactive journal of self-exploration, offering a Buddhist practice of meditation. ***Welcoming the Unwelcome: Wholehearted Living in a Brokenhearted World*** (Shambhala October 8, 2019) by the same author reminds us that everything we say and do leaves an imprint.

Transcendental Meditation is a Hindu-based meditation practice. More information is available through the website www.TM.org.

Holographic Leadership

There are a great many books that discuss values-based leadership. Greenleaf and Burns themselves could fill an entire page. ***The Power of Servant Leadership*** (Berrett-Koehler Publishers; 1st edition, September 4, 1998) by Robert Greenleaf and ***Transforming Leadership***, (Grove Press; Reprint edition, January 30, 2004) by James McGregor Burns are two seminal books and a place to start if you are interested in the foundational ideas and the basis for an emerging field of leadership studies, applied in business.

David Bohm's work is critical to understanding our interconnection and the impact that changing our assumptions has on us individually and as a collective. Wholeness changes all the rules of interaction. For our story, we drew on Bohm's ***Wholeness and the Implicate Order*** (Routledge; 1st edition, July 4, 2002), ***Thought as a System*** (Routledge; 1st edition, December 2, 1994), and ***On Dialogue*** (Routledge; 2nd edition, September 1, 2004).

In 1980, Joseph Jaworski had the privilege to interview David Bohm and integrated ideas from quantum physics into his life's work. His bestselling book ***Synchronicity: The Inner Path of Leadership*** (Berrett-Koehler Publishers; 1st edition, January 1, 1996) is an inspirational guide illustrating the most essential leadership capacity: developing our being and our consciousness to enable shifts in how we see the world, understand relationships, and make commitments. Expanding upon the ideas in *Synchronicity*, Jaworski wrote ***Source: The Inner Path of Knowledge Creation*** (Berrett-Koehler Publishers; 1st edition, February 10, 2012), which takes its readers on an extraordinarily wide-ranging intellectual odyssey with quantum physicists, cognitive scientists, indigenous leaders, and spiritual thinkers—all focused on getting to the heart of what it means to connect to Source and those moments when extreme spontaneity and intuitive insight occur.

The Human Phenomenon (Sussex Academic Press; Edition Unstated, September 1, 1999) by Pierre Teilhard de Chardin, translation by Sarah Appleton-Weber, is a powerful book and, in reality, a slow read.

Margaret Wheatley's ***Leadership and the New Science*** (Berrett-Koehler Publishers; 3rd edition, September 3, 2006) is a groundbreaking work that introduced the new science within a frame of values-based leadership.

In ***Presence: Human Purpose and the Field of the Future*** (Crown Business; 1st edition, August 16, 2005), Peter Senge, Joseph Jaworski, C. Otto Scharmer, and Betty Sue Flowers share their experience with field dynamics and Wholeness. They reveal how our own presence affects our lives and those around us. This book encourages us to allow our inner knowing to emerge so we may then act swiftly with a natural flow.

Peter Senge's ***The Fifth Discipline: The Art & Practice of the Learning Organization***, (Doubleday, Revised & Updated edition, March 21, 2006), introduced the concept of mental models into organizational leadership. He explained the need to suspend and allow our deeply ingrained assumptions and generalizations that influence how we understand the world and how we act. He helped us begin to see how we are not consciously aware of our mental models or the effects they have on our behavior. He discusses how leaders can become more actively self-aware and commit to building learning organizations—companies that ease the learning of all stakeholders, and continuously transforming themselves.

Leadership Without Easy Answers (Harvard University Press; 1st edition, July 22, 1998) by Ronald Heifetz and ***The Practice of Adaptive Leadership*** (Harvard Business Review Press; 1st edition, May 18, 2009) by Ronald Heifetz, Alexander Grashow, and Marty

Linksy provide the understanding of the tasks of leadership Marie (Gertrude) and Laura used.

The research that clarifies the components of a toxic culture comes from ***Toxic Workplace: Managing Toxic Personalities and Their Systems of Power*** by Mitchell Kusy and Elizabeth Holloway (Jossey-Bass; 1st edition, March 27, 2009).

Jan Byars' dissertation, ***Holographic Leadership: Leading as a Way of Being*** (published as Janet Byars), brought these works together and offers a new model of practice for organizations looking to work from interconnection and own their impact within the world. Connect with Jan at www.JanByars.com. Jan also has guided meditations available on *Insight Timer*.

Other Notable Works

Parker Palmer, ***A Hidden Wholeness: The Journey Toward an Undivided Life***

(Blackstone Audio, 2009) and ***An Undivided Life: Seeking Wholeness in Ourselves, Our Work, and Our World*** (Audible, Sounds True, 2015).

Duncan Coombe, ***Can You Really Power an Organization with Love?*** (Harvard Business Review Press, August 1, 2016).

Judy Cannato, ***Field of Compassion: How the New Cosmology Is Transforming Spiritual Life*** (Sorin Books; March 8, 2010).

Edgar Schein, ***Organizational Culture and Leadership*** (Wiley; 5th edition (December 27, 2016).

MaryBeth Hyland, ***Permission to Be Human: The Conscious Leader's Guide to Creating a Values-Driven Culture*** (SparkVision Publishing (June 9, 2021).

The Bohm-Krishnamurti Project: Exploring the Legacy of the David Bohm and Jiddu Krishnamurti Relationship may be accessed at the website www.bohmkrishnamurti.com.

C. Otto Scharmer, ***The Essentials of Theory U*** (Berrett-Koehler Publishers, March 20, 2018) offers an expanded view of organizational change. Otto's work integrates David Bohm's work as Theory U is best used from a coherent physical state.

Lynn McTaggart, ***The Field: The Quest for the Secret Force of the Universe*** (HarperPerennial; updated ed. edition, January 2, 2008).

Michael Talbot, ***The Holographic Universe: The Revolutionary Theory of Reality*** (HarperPerennial; Reprint edition, September 6, 2011). Building on the work of David Bohm, Talbot offers a deeper view of a holographic universe.

Amit Goswami, ***The Self-Aware Universe: How Consciousness Creates the Material World*** (TarcherPerigee, March 21, 1995).

Sarah Hill, ***The Tao of Dialogue*** (Routledge; 1st edition, March 26, 2019). Sarah helps us to understand more about how to leverage dialogic principles in managing relationships within the workplace.

Master Lam Kam-Chuen, ***The Way of Energy: Mastering the Chinese Art of Internal Strength with Qigong Exercise*** (Simon & Schuster Inc.; 1st edition, November 15, 1991).

Appendix B: Outline of Process

These steps are written in a linear fashion. Linearity was built into our language. However, these steps are not linear; they will overlap, cross over, and shift. What's important is that they build on and strengthen each other. Start within yourself. Build your core capacity before you move out into the organization with these ideas.

1. **Release the sense of overwhelm**. The realization that gutting it out isn't working; some would call this hitting bottom.

2. **Move—exercise**. Get out of your head. Break the spinning mind by burning off the stress chemicals and becoming more balanced and centered in your body.

3. **Manage your own state**. Begin to be aware of all the emotions you have shoved down inside. You may need help with this. It's better to have support.

4. **Begin to look for opportunity**. For the ladies that was drawing on their leadership training and the books that they have read to find another way.

5. **Vision and values**. You may have this or you may need to create it. Build this as a team with as much input as you can.

6. **Silence or mindfulness.** Begin with what appeals to you, disengage the spinning mind.

7. **Find support.** A person or people who will show up with you. It can of course be done alone, begin where you are. The support may come at a different time.

8. **Intention.** Create this together with those who are joining you. Let it sit for a while and revise, as necessary.

9. **Conviction and intention.** Be clear on what you are creating, committing to the discipline that it requires. Finding ways, no matter how small, to move toward intention.

10. **Deepen your capacity.** Iterate, keep going with these steps, and they will build traction and hope. Be aware of you own level of psychological development and move to expand your capacity. Add additional skills in meditation or a mindfulness skill you can use in the moment, deepening your stillness. Be kind to yourself.

11. **Celebrate the victories, big and small!** Appreciate your own efforts; appreciate those who have joined you. Do this often!

12. **Listen and suspend.** Use your newfound clarity to open to possibility and listen to all the voices. There is a great depth of knowledge here.

13. **Begin to move out into your organization.** From internal coherence comes deeper insight into issues in your organization. Solve some of the obvious issues, low-hanging fruit.

14. **Dialogue.** Begin to introduce ideas within safe groups.

15. **Stay with it.** Allow the process to build and take you to the next step, based in coherence and critical thinking. Watch for flow. Allow the momentum, aligned with intention and values.

The ladies used this intention: *"To work from Wholeness and interconnection; sensing and knowing there is a solution embedded within every problem. Be responsible for our own internal state and the impact we have on the organization. Commit to our own development and bring ourselves back into coherence, moment to moment. Support each other through this process. Silence and mindfulness builds our internal capacity as we move out into the organization. Step out of our limited self into an expanding sense of Wholeness."*

Appendix C: Glossary

Attention refers to the object of conscious awareness, the selection of focus. When we chose to focus on one thing we lose focus on others. It is a powerful choice.

The **autonomic nervous system** is a critical part of our body controlling involuntary physical processes such as our fight-or-flight reaction. It plays a big role in how frantic or coherent we are and what memories get triggered.

Coherence can be used in both a physiological and system meaning of the word. For an individual, it refers to clarity of thought and emotional balance. For a system, it refers to the synchronization between multiple systems. A laser has a high level of phase or frequency lock.

In organizations, high levels of coherence allow the emergence of creativity, cooperation, and productivity.

Global coherence is coherence where the distinctive parts generate an emergent whole that is greater than the sum of the individual parts. This can also referred to as *synchronization*.

Psychophysiological coherence. The HeartMath Institute identifies this as a more organized electromagnetic heart field.

Incoherence, for individuals, means having inconsistent, fragmented, and unclear thoughts that are hard to understand. For organizations, incoherence is a similar lack of clarity and consistency on a larger scale.

Emergence is the transformation of energy and information, potential moving into possibility across time/space. It is a process where complex systems self-organize into novel and coherent patterns. Emergence involves something coming into matter (physical reality) as a result of the collection of the whole, rather than any individual state.

Emergent knowledge is the insight and creativity that comes to each of us as we release our frantic thoughts, holding a clear, coherence state and allowing Wholeness to shape our thoughts and actions.

Entrainment is similar to coherence and synchronization, where systems are pulled into the same rhythm by the strongest rhythm that can lead to the emergence of complex, synchronized behavior.

A **field** is an energy dynamic within the universe. Rupert Sheldrake tells us that fields interrelate and interconnect energy and matter. Fields do not have form; instead, matter is energy bound within fields.

A **bioenergetic field** is an electromagnetic field generated by all animals. For humans, the main sources of this field are the heart and brain.

A **field group** is a group that consciously holds the intention of an organization through the practices that make up holographic leadership.

A **heart field** is an energetic field emitted by our heart that extends up to fifteen feet (as currently measured) from the body. An extension of this field is the **HeartMind**. This is the integrated functioning of the leader, including their bioenergetic fields, which, when in a stable coherent state, offers a greater possibility of global coherence for the group.

Heart wisdom is emergent knowledge, insight, and intuition; wisdom that emerges through a coherent heart.

A **holding environment** is a psychosocial environment very similar to that which is referenced by the word *culture*. It is understood to be adaptable and can be shifted into a healthier state. A holding environment in business is a relationship where one has the capacity to direct and hold the attention of their people to facilitate productive work. In holographic leadership, a holding environment also recognizes an energetic field of possibility and represents the primary conditions of emergence for an organization.

Holographic leadership is leadership that works from the model of quantum Wholeness. This model suggests that by getting the Whole into an entrained balance, its various parts fall into place. It assumes interconnection and that with clear, integrous, conscious intention and a coherent state one can draw from the quantum probabilities in accord with the intentions of the group.

Integrity is alignment; the degree to which the organization holds to its defined vision, values, and intention; the expression of real values. It encompasses the behavior and professed values of the group. By defining the level of commitment, the level of integrity also defines the organization's ability to change and the type of change that is possible. In our story, integrity was assumed to have a group or system focus, to be beneficial for the Whole. In this context, it transcends the focus on "me," which is more much present in the command-and-control model of leadership.

Intention is the guiding power of the organization. Intention shapes reality by shaping people's perception. It is the basis or vision that gives a framework to an organization's mission and values and provides a reference point for the leader.

Mental models represent the personal assumptions from which we make decisions. They have a profound influence on how we understand the world and the actions we take. They are for the most part unconscious, having little awareness of their effects on our behavior.

Quantum-holographic theory is a theory of physics that discusses how information is processed. Holographic fields are based on a field concept of order, meaning information of the whole system is enfolded into the field and distributed to all of its parts.

Suspending (opinions, judgment, and assumptions) is a critical skill of self-awareness, suggested by Bohm and embodying the essence of cognitive-behavioral theory. As we become more aware of our underlying assumptions, we have the power to shift them, allowing us to see ourselves and others more clearly.

Sustained incoherence is a state where we are so consistently off balance (out of coherence), that our thoughts and knowledge become automatic so we are largely controlled by them. With this automation, we lose much of our authenticity and freedom.

Undivided Wholeness is a concept discussed by David Bohm. Wholeness is an energetic interconnected field of which we are part, which includes our response (whether it is coherent or fragmented) to our interaction with it. It moves beyond the frame of me/we/world.

Values-based leadership is an evolution in leadership theory that began in the late 1970s. It is built on ideas such as self-reflection, balance, humility, and the common good.

Wholeness is a concept discussed at length by David Bohm. A view from Wholeness is an understanding of an interconnected energy field of which we are part (*see* Undivided Wholeness.)

Index

A

Active self-awareness 111
Attention 4, 5, 11, 13, 23, 24, 26, 30,
    38, 40, 41, 49, 53, 55, 67, 74,
    76, 77, 80, 81, 85, 88, 89, 103,
    110, 111, 118, 119, 120, 126,
    127, 130, 137, 145, 147
Autonomic nervous system 37, 41,
    65, 81, 86, 116, 121, 145

B

Bohm, David xiii, xvii, xviii, xix,
    xxi, xxii, xxiv, 8, 9, 15, 20, 34,
    124, 128, 129, 135, 138, 141,
    148, 149
Breathe 24
Business xvi, xviii, xix, xxi, 4, 28, 38,
    39, 41, 43, 51, 62, 75, 85, 89,
    90, 109, 110, 126, 127, 129,
    130, 131, 132, 136, 138, 139,
    140, 147

C

Calm 9, 12, 14, 17, 31, 33, 37, 45, 47,
    53, 61, 69, 70, 73, 76, 78, 80,
    83, 86, 117, 118, 126, 135

Coherence xiii, xxiii, 23, 27, 33, 37,
    40, 44, 45, 46, 47, 49, 55, 62,
    66, 71, 74, 75, 82, 85, 86, 101,
    109, 110, 112, 113, 125, 127,
    128, 135, 136, 143, 144, 145,
    146, 147, 148
Consciousness 26, 40, 47, 72, 103,
    119, 125, 136, 138, 141
Critical thinking 28, 34, 42, 67, 69,
    111, 117, 125, 144
Culture xviii, 38, 39, 41, 42, 49, 61,
    72, 75, 76, 79, 83, 84, 100,
    101, 111, 123, 127, 130, 131,
    140, 141, 147

D

Decision-making 84, 126
Dialogue xviii, xix, xxiv, 47, 48, 49,
    50, 66, 76, 86, 87, 88, 90, 91,
    92, 93, 97, 112, 117, 125, 126,
    128, 129, 130, 138, 141, 143

E

EFT (see emotional freedom
    technique) 71, 116, 117, 136
Emergence 145, 146, 147

Emotional freedom technique
  (EFT) 71, 116, 117, 136
Emotional intelligence 15, 27, 28,
  72, 111, 121
Entrainment 146

F

Field xix, xxii, 9, 10, 26, 29, 32, 34,
  41, 42, 52, 56, 59, 109, 110,
  112, 123, 124, 125, 126, 127,
  129, 132, 138, 139, 140, 141,
  145, 146, 147, 148, 149

H

Healing 38, 48, 119, 121
Holding the environment 47
Holographic 20, 26, 60, 65, 66, 73,
  98, 112, 113, 117, 118, 119,
  123, 124, 125, 126, 127, 129,
  130, 131, 132, 133, 138, 140,
  141, 146, 147, 148

I

Inner state 113, 126, 129, 130
Intention xxiv, 5, 12, 21, 22, 23, 25,
  26, 27, 28, 29, 30, 39, 40, 43,
  44, 45, 58, 65, 67, 71, 72, 74,
  75, 76, 81, 84, 85, 88, 91, 95,
  100, 102, 105, 112, 115, 119,
  122, 126, 128, 130, 137, 143,
  144, 146, 147, 148
Intuition 46, 69, 81, 102, 111, 131,
  136, 147

L

Leadership xviii, xix, 4, 5, 10, 15, 19,
  22, 24, 25, 27, 37, 39, 41, 42,
  43, 44, 45, 47, 48, 49, 50, 52,
  53, 54, 56, 57, 60, 61, 64, 65,
  66, 68, 72, 73, 75, 76, 77, 79,
  81, 83, 90, 97, 98, 101, 109,
  110, 111, 112, 113, 116, 117,
  118, 119, 121, 123, 124, 125,
  126, 127, 129, 130, 131, 132,
  133, 135, 136, 138, 139, 140,
  142, 146, 147, 149
Listen xxiv, 14, 47, 55, 62, 69, 77,
  79, 81, 88, 89, 91, 97, 111,
  117, 118, 123, 126, 128, 129,
  130, 143

M

Meditation 9, 27, 31, 37, 38, 45, 66,
  82, 85, 118, 136, 137, 140, 143
Mindfulness 50, 66, 74, 78, 86,
  93, 98, 115, 130, 135, 136,
  143, 144

O

Organizational development xix

P

Peace xxii, 7, 8, 9, 10, 18, 21, 23,
  24, 40, 46, 48, 59, 79, 86, 96,
  102, 110
Personal development 119
Possibility xxi, 11, 29, 30, 34, 47, 65,
  110, 121, 124, 131, 132, 143,
  146, 147
Practice xix, xx, 24, 28, 35, 36, 38,
  39, 44, 45, 48, 49, 66, 72, 75,
  77, 81, 82, 84, 85, 87, 88, 90,
  92, 93, 95, 96, 97, 98, 101, 110,
  115, 117, 118, 120, 121, 123,
  127, 128, 130, 131, 132, 135,
  137, 139, 140, 146

Prayer 85, 96, 118, 137
Presence 62, 79, 86, 93, 97, 102, 103, 104, 122, 137, 139
Purpose xvii, xix, 10, 64, 101, 112, 118, 119, 123, 128, 132, 139

Q

Qigong 117, 141

R

Relationship xix, xxii, 10, 72, 111, 138, 141, 147

S

Self-care 102, 110, 111
Shadow 109
Shared meaning xiii, 93, 128, 130
Silence 10, 12, 17, 35, 38, 40, 46, 48, 50, 60, 66, 74, 78, 81, 82, 85, 86, 88, 89, 90, 92, 93, 96, 97, 98, 103, 118, 130, 131, 135, 137, 143, 144
Spirituality 136
Stillness 17, 88, 118, 143
Sustained incoherence 14, 124, 148
Synchronicity xiii, xviii, 42, 43, 60, 100, 104, 138

T

Teilhard de Chardin, Pierre 124, 125, 139
Toxicity 6, 7, 23, 24, 25, 26, 27, 30, 34, 40, 41, 45, 57, 63, 67, 69, 70, 71, 77, 85, 113, 116, 128, 132
Transformation xviii, xxii, xxiv, 38, 41, 102, 146

U

Universe xx, 5, 7, 15, 63, 103, 104, 105, 124, 125, 132, 141, 146

V

Values xix, 5, 10, 15, 27, 28, 36, 37, 39, 42, 43, 50, 57, 62, 64, 65, 66, 72, 75, 76, 77, 79, 84, 98, 100, 102, 112, 118, 119, 123, 124, 126, 127, 128, 132, 138, 139, 141, 142, 144, 147, 148, 149
Visionary 112
Vulnerability 90, 121

W

Wellbeing 48, 110, 135
Wholeness xiii, xviii, xix, xx, xxi, xxii, xxiii, xxiv, 6, 7, 10, 11, 12, 15, 20, 21, 23, 24, 25, 26, 27, 28, 30, 31, 32, 34, 36, 37, 38, 40, 41, 45, 49, 58, 59, 60, 63, 65, 66, 71, 74, 75, 76, 79, 80, 81, 84, 86, 91, 94, 96, 100, 103, 104, 105, 109, 110, 115, 117, 118, 120, 124, 125, 127, 137, 138, 139, 140, 144, 146, 147, 148, 149

Contact Us

Check out our book page at **ACalltoWholeness.com**

Jan Byars, PhD, can be contacted through her websites: JanByars.com and LeadSyncNow.com.

Please sign up for her updates, emails, and events! Jan is available for individual and group development, training, HeartMath coaching, and speaking engagements.

Like and follow Jan on social media.
Linked In: http://www.linkedin.com/in/jbyars
Facebook: https://www.facebook.com/Dr-Jan-Byars-at-LeadSync-129446573800342/
HeartMath: https://certified.heartmath.com/user/jan-byars/
Twitter: https://twitter.com/drjanbyars

Susan Taylor can be contacted through her websites: GeneronInternational.com and DialogueCreates.com

Susan is available for individual, team, and organizational transformational renewal, underpinned by Dialogue.

Like and follow Susan on social media.
Linked In: https://www.linkedin.com/in/susan-taylor-transformative-leadership-coach/
Twitter: Susan Taylor (@TayloredWisdom) / Twitter

About the Authors

Jan Byars holds transformational space. She has integrated multiple fields of study into a distinctly innovative approach that encompasses the whole person and the organization. She has a PhD in Leadership and Change, a MS in Clinical Counseling, a Licensed Professional Clinical Counselor, and a professional certified HeartMath coach. Jan lives in Indianapolis, IN and has a dog that looks a lot like DB.

Susan Taylor is a transformational coach and consultant who has worked with some of the most renowned thought leaders in the domains of emotional, spiritual and leadership intelligence for more than 25 years. She helps clients fulfill their deeper purpose by fostering creative and inspiring business environments that support people to learn, grow and thrive while delivering extraordinary results. Susan possesses a deep passion and expertise in Dialogue. Specifically, Bohmian Dialogue. This has proven to lead to new and deeper understandings, resulting in profound transformations.